CENTURY OF SERVICE 1902-2002

OGE Energy Corp.

Our First 100 Years
1902–2002

THE
DONNING COMPANY
PUBLISHERS

Mustang Power Plant during a turbine overhaul.

The Donning Company Publishers
184 Business Park Drive, Suite 206
Virginia Beach, VA 23462-6533

Steve Mull, General Manager
Ed Williams, Project Director
Debbie Williams, Project Research Coordinator
Dawn V. Kofroth, Assistant General Manager
Richard A. Horwege, Senior Editor
E. M. McClure, Senior Graphic Designer
John Harrell, Imaging Artist
Scott Rule, Director of Marketing
Gigi Abbott, Marketing Coordinator

Library of Congress Cataloging-in-Publication Data
Morris, Robert R., 1946–
    OGE Energy Corp.: our first 100 years, 1902–2002 / by Robert R. Morris.
       p. cm.
    Includes index.
    ISBN 1-57864-157-8 (alk. paper)
    1. OGE Energy Corp.—History. 2. Electric utilities—Oklahoma—History. 3. Gas companies—Oklahoma—History. I. OGE Energy Corp. II. Title.

HD9685.U7 O555 2002
333.793'2'09766—dc21

2001058154

Printed in the United States of America

Contents

Frank Keating
Governor

HAPPY 100TH BIRTHDAY TO THE OG&E FAMILY!

Oklahoma will celebrate its statehood centennial in 2007 -- but OG&E beat us to it!

As one of Oklahoma's original companies, OG&E has served the vital power needs of our people for 100 years. From an era when electricity was a rare luxury to a new millennium where electric-powered communication spans the globe at the speed of light, OG&E has provided energy to build, to grow, to prosper and to thrive. Yours is a company with a single goal: service. You can take pride, as members of the OG&E family, in the fact that you provide a universal service that is almost taken for granted by Oklahomans -- especially in an era when many other regions of our country are concerned about energy shortages and crises.

As Governor, I have had a number of occasions to see OG&E professionals in action at times when your Oklahoma neighbors needed help. In all weather conditions, in the wake of some frightening and tragic natural disasters, OG&E has been there, restoring power and normal life with skill and compassion. It is a mark of your professionalism that most Oklahomans never notice what you do on a daily basis.

OG&E is also a fine corporate citizen, offering support to a myriad of civic, community and arts organizations that enrich our lives. For 100 years, you have been the best; Happy Birthday, OG&E. We appreciate you!

Sincerely,

Frank Keating

STATE OF ARKANSAS
OFFICE OF THE GOVERNOR
State Capitol
Little Rock 72201

Mike Huckabee
Governor

December 14, 2001

OGE Energy Corp.
P.O. Box 321
Oklahoma City, OK 73101

Greetings:

Congratulations on 100 years of service to your customers. You've been an important, reliable source of energy and employment for people in Oklahoma and western Arkansas. The key to success has been a dedicated workforce that has maintained a steadfast adherence to quality service.

This is quite a milestone in the history of the company. We're proud Arkansas has been part of your history since the mid 1920s. Congratulations and keep up the good work.

Sincerely yours,

Mike Huckabee

MH:st

OGE Energy Corp.   PO Box 321
Oklahoma City, Oklahoma 73101-0321
405-553-3000
www.oge.com

OG+E

Happy Anniversary!

At OGE Energy Corp., we're celebrating 100 years in business. It's a big milestone for us, and we want to share with you the story of how we got here. We think you'll find it interesting and informative, and believe you'll agree that we're really just getting started.

Since our company was founded in 1902, five years before Oklahoma became the 46th state, OGE has served as an important and reliable source of energy here in America's heartland. Pioneers built this company — and along with it, helped to build a new state. It has been a century of constant growth and rapid change, but one thing remains the same: Day in and day out, our people deliver high-quality service.

This fact has been recognized many times over the years. The national Utility of the Year Award in 1983 comes to mind. We've been named to the Forbes Magazine Platinum List of America's Best Big Companies two years in a row. We've joined the Fortune 500, and we've won the nation's highest honor for disaster recovery, the Edison Electric Institute Emergency Response Award.

Resource Data International, the gold standard for power plant evaluation, routinely ranks our Sooner and Muskogee generating stations among the most cost-efficient in North America. We've been recognized many times for our work to protect the environment we all share. We've grown a pipeline originally built to serve our gas-fired plants into a natural gas gathering, processing and transmission system ranked among the nation's 10 largest. And the list goes on.

This commemorative book captures the highlights of our first century of service, as we prepare to compete in the energy market of America's future. It is offered as a sincere thank-you to OGE Energy Corp. members past and present, to our customers and the communities we serve.

Sincerely,

Steven Moore

Steven E. Moore
Chairman, President and Chief Executive Officer

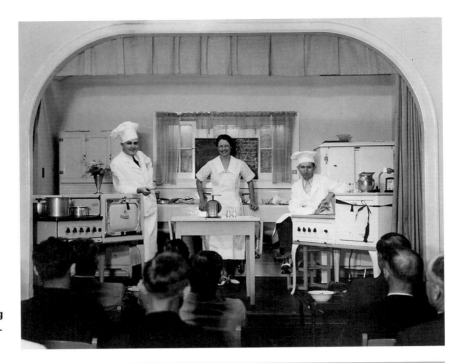

Members take a break during a cooking demonstration featuring electric appliances.

OGE Energy Corp.'s Place in History

In 1902:

- Theodore Roosevelt is the popular president of the United States, and a New York department store starts selling "teddy bears" in his honor.

- Inventor Willis H. Carrier first demonstrates air conditioning as a practical electrical appliance.

- The International Harvester Company is founded by Cyrus McCormick Jr. with financial backing from J. P. Morgan.

- Edwin Binney of Easton, Pennsylvania, introduces Crayola brand crayons.

- James Cash Penney opens a retail store called the Golden Rule in Kemmerer, Wyoming. Later, the company would be called J. C. Penney.

- The National Biscuit Company first markets Animal Crackers.

- North Carolina pharmacist Caleb Bradham founds Pepsi-Cola.

- James Drummond Dole starts the Hawaiian Pineapple Company, Ltd.

- The Twentieth Century Limited train sets a speed record, zipping from New York to Chicago in twenty hours.

- The First Tournament of Roses football game is held in Pasadena, California.

- **OGE Energy Corp. begins as Oklahoma Gas and Electric Company in Oklahoma City.**

Introduction

This story describes a century of hardworking, proud, and dedicated people. They brought the wonders of the modern era to the settlers of Oklahoma and western Arkansas. Throughout their history, the members of OGE Energy Corp. flourished on change and the compelling need to find new and better ways to serve customers.

One of the most notable changes in the company's history took place in 1995 as the company chose a new name. In a response to the coming era of electric utility deregulation, OGE Energy Corp. was formed. The new holding company combined the traditional regulated utility company with unregulated ventures in natural gas production, processing, and transportation as well as energy marketing.

For more than ninety years, this company was known as the Oklahoma Gas and Electric Company, or simply "OG&E." For consistency throughout this book, we refer to the company as OG&E prior to 1996. Following the changeover, we refer to the company in most instances as OGE Energy Corp.

Admittedly, not everyone can make this jump easily. For thousands of people, we remain what we've always been called—"OG&E."

The overwhelming majority of resources for this book were obtained from the large and well-documented archives of OGE Energy Corp., located at the company's headquarters in Oklahoma City.

The newest addition to the OG&E fleet of vehicles is the serial number 0100-bucket truck in observance of the company's one hundredth anniversary. The bucket truck is an International 4000 Series.

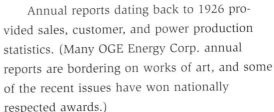

Annual reports dating back to 1926 provided sales, customer, and power production statistics. (Many OGE Energy Corp. annual reports are bordering on works of art, and some of the recent issues have won nationally respected awards.)

Individual and bound copies of the in-house magazine *The Meter* from as early as 1921 (when it was the weekly publication *The Oklahoma Meter*) gave wonderful human-interest insight into the company and the people who built it. Particularly valuable were retrospectives contained in issues of the *Meter* upon the company's fiftieth anniversary in 1952, as well as the ninetieth in 1992.

Innumerable issues of *Inside* and *Inside OG&E*, regular informational newsletters for employees, enhanced understanding of many of the operational intricacies of OGE Energy Corp. and the utility industry.

Hours of interviews with longtime company members "filled in the blanks" of this story, giving it a human face.

Boxes of historical information, correspondences, advertisements, and promotional material were made available and reviewed. Drawers filling a wall of file cabinets contained an awe-inspiring assortment of historical photographs and slides.

The early years of the company's history would be lost were it not for George Steinmeyer's "A History of the Oklahoma Gas and Electric Company to the Year 1912," an unpublished but nonetheless extremely valuable thesis for his master's degree at the University of Oklahoma.

Michelle Madden, meter technician, Enid Meter Department.

Left: Sooner Power Plant.

Completed in 1961, this landmark work is our only documented link to the ancestor companies (and people who formed them) preceding OG&E, and the rollicking first decade of the company's history.

All of this historical material was managed and made available to the author by Beverly Bennett, communications specialist of OGE Energy's Corporate Communications Department. Beverly was clear, concise, and extremely helpful in expectations for this project.

Finally, all the staff at OGE Energy quietly exudes a sense of positive accomplishment and pride for their company, while at the same time working from a vantage point of courtesy and hospitality.

—Robert R. Morris
July 2001

Phil Crissup, senior engineer, Power Delivery.

The award-winning Formula Lightning electric racecar sponsored by OGE Energy Corp. and the University of Oklahoma.

"We've demonstrated our ability to get the job done and as new challenges arise, you can expect us to confront them head on."

**OGE Energy Corp.
1999 Annual Report**

CHAPTER 1

Members

The 100-year history of OGE Energy Corp. contains hundreds of milestones, accomplishments and contributions benefiting the people of Oklahoma and western Arkansas. The company's strength has been built upon the people who work day by day as OGE Energy members.

OG&E member Sylvester Davis had it. So does Richard Kitchens. Gilbert Hall has it, too. And so does Esperanza Hughes. Entire OG&E departments have it.

It's called pride.

Sylvester Davis walked up to a crowd standing around a young boy who had been injured and was bleeding from a neck wound. Pushing his way through, Davis immediately put pressure on the artery and continued with first aid until the paramedics arrived. Davis saved the young boy's life.

Davis was an OG&E meter reader from the 1920s through the 1940s. His supervisors awarded him the OG&E Medal for his heroism. Yet there was more to Davis. In twenty-one years on the job, he was never off schedule, never out of meter book sequence, and never had a recorded driving accident.

Davis thought he had the best job in the world. He acted like it.

Sylvester Davis had pride.

Richard Kitchens is a senior engineer for Enogex, Inc. Kitchens volunteers as a tutor in an elementary school. He devotes one lunch hour per week in a school with many students who come from poor homes.

One of Kitchens' students did not show up for a session—the boy's home had burned down during the night, a total loss. Kitchens immediately asked for donations from fellow Enogex members. The response was overwhelming, and was matched by a company gift. His help, together with that of his co-workers, put the family back on its feet.

Richard Kitchens has pride, too.

Gilbert Hall is training coordinator at the Muskogee Power Plant. Besides his critical work as a company member, Hall is deeply involved in the economic development of the Muskogee community. Recognized as one of the most influential people in Muskogee, Hall spends countless

Environmental Training and Safety staff members (left to right) John Solenberg, training specialist; Ervin Warren, supervisor; and Harry McRee, training specialist.

Ann Perryman, representative, Power Contracts, Power Supply.

Richard Kitchens, senior engineer at Enogex, tutors a student at Shidler Elementary School.

volunteer hours promoting the community, assisting in economic and social development, and constantly promoting diversification and minority business development. It is his passion.

"You can't get involved in a community's development with the mindset of 'what's in it for me,'" Hall says modestly. "You have to do it for the community, and spend time doing the important things."

Hall recognized that a great community is built by the people in it. He also realizes that as an OGE Energy member, he has a civic responsibility.

He does it with pride.

Esperanza Hughes is a distribution operator. Her job often requires her to work nights for Power Delivery. When trouble strikes—as it does so regularly given the frequency of storms in Oklahoma and western Arkansas—Hughes must instantly field emergency calls. She then must quickly—and flawlessly—explain the cause and extent of the emergency or problem to a field crew or to the OGE Energy spokesman on call, who then relays updated information to the media.

Hughes never misses a beat. It's part of the territory. She's proud of her work.

Groups of OGE members show pride whenever disaster strikes, whenever customers are in danger or simply deprived of their power, even for the shortest time. OGE pride was never greater than during the immediate minutes and days following the Alfred P. Murrah Federal Building bombing in 1995. OGE members rushed to cut power where it was a danger, to restore power where it had been severed, and to assist anyone in need during the foggy aftermath of horror.

Throughout the company's history, Oklahoma and western Arkansas have been the focus of many storms, including disastrous tornadoes and deadly floods. Members have left family and safety to give a helping hand, save a life, and restore power as quickly as possible. Such behavior is legend.

A Century of Pride

From OG&E's start in the wild and raw Oklahoma Territory in 1902 through the decades to today, the bold theme of pride

Bottom: Mike Hill, telephone customer service consultant.

Van Nguyen, payroll assistant, Corporate Services.

runs through company members.

It was seen in the tenuous early days when the lights flickered as financiers bickered.

It was apparent in their reactions to storms, economic emergencies, wartime, and drought.

It was observed during the last quarter of the twentieth century as OGE Energy dramatically changed with the multiple pressures facing the electric industry.

OGE Energy members' pride was clearly noticed, when in 1996, the company restructured into business units—to launch into a twenty-first century world of increased competition.

The OGE Energy of 2002 is almost unrecognizable when compared to the Oklahoma Gas and Electric Company of 1902. Today, OGE Energy is a member of the *Fortune* 500 list of the nation's biggest and the *Forbes* Platinum 400 list of the nation's best companies. OGE Energy's business takes place both in

regulated and nonregulated spheres. Its power plants have repeatedly received national awards as being among the most efficient power-producing utilities in the land.

The company has been successful for one hundred years. That success is the result of hard work originating from a sound, winning strategy. That strategy includes a commitment to operational excellence, disciplined growth, readiness for customer choice, and developing new skills. Each OGE Energy member participates in and fulfills the winning strategy.

Though much has changed since 1902, the thread of member pride, there at the start, continues today. OGE Energy is a company of people who have spent ten decades serving in roles destined to make it a great company. Its people have made OGE Energy what it is today. ■

Ruth Bondoni, clerk-typist, Market Solutions.

Top: Arkansas division workers.

Facing page, top: Ted Randle, engineering tech, Power Delivery.
Facing page, bottom: Karen Goodner, lead operator, Transmission and Delivery Control Center, Metro.

> *"OG&E employees are expected to question if they are doing a job right, and if they are doing the right job. It's the result of the company's ongoing Quality Process."*

OGE Energy Corp.
1993 Annual Report

CHAPTER 2

Lighting the Way to the Future: 1889–1903

Oklahoma City sprang up overnight as thousands of land-hungry settlers poured in to stake their homestead claims in 1889. The railroad tent village grew to become the capital of the nation's forty-sixth state (inset).

From its very start in the 1889 Land Run, Oklahoma City residents wanted dependable sources of water as well as the wildly popular electric lights. Several entrepreneurial companies tried —and failed. One company would eventually emerge as the champion of Oklahoma electrification.

Even before Oklahoma City was called that (the tiny settlement started as a depot called Oklahoma Station on the Sante Fe Railroad line in 1887)—the early residents demanded a regular supply of water. If the town were to flourish and prosper, it would also need the new electric power harnessed by storied inventor Thomas Edison.

An Imaginative Plan Doomed to Failure

In 1890, the Oklahoma City Council awarded Quincy, Illinois transplant C. W. Price a franchise to operate two important ventures—the Oklahoma Ditch and Water Power Company and the Oklahoma City Light and Power Company.

The idea was ambitious: to build a six-mile canal, diverting water from the North Canadian River into Oklahoma City. The canal would provide a regular fresh water source and a means to generate electric power. It failed.

Price convinced others to buy stock and once granted a franchise, began a monumental engineering task for the 1890s. Dozens of workers dug a ten-foot-deep trench, thirty-two feet wide at the top. Water powered a modest electric generating station at Robinson Avenue and Frisco Street.

The Light That Didn't Last

Virtually all of Oklahoma City's four thousand residents turned out for the ceremonial lighting of the first lamps on Christmas Eve, 1890. After appropriate speechmaking and gushing praise by city leaders heaped upon those who brought progress to the city, a dignitary threw the switch and the first light bulbs flickered on—primarily in the power plant.

Then they flickered off. Then they stayed off. The people went

Oklahoma City's first power-generating plant included a dynamo and two generators. Total capacity could illuminate fifteen hundred light bulbs.

Right: An ill-fated attempt to divert river water into a canal to power the first electric plant failed when the water percolated into the sandy soil, leaving the power turbines silent and the city dark.

home, lit candles or kerosene lamps, and put the party hats away. The lights never came back on—at least in this venture.

It seems the canal's sandy bottom simply allowed the diverted water to percolate away into the dry subsoil. The new canal evaporated. So did the ability to generate electricity.

Oklahoma Ditch and Water Power Company, together with Oklahoma City Light and Power went belly up. Price, despite repeated attempts to get the power going again through other means including steam power, never saw his dream become a reality. He died in 1892.

More Starts and Stops

The failure to provide power to Oklahoma City did not reduce the need. Other schemes came and went over the next several years.

In 1893, the newly formed Oklahoma City Gas Company set about installing gaslights throughout the city. Simultaneously, the late C. W. Price's brother Seymour gathered his brother's assets and those of other investors and mounted a reconstituted Oklahoma City Light and Power Company.

For a while, both utilities operated side-by-side, with electric lights and gaslights illuminating the city—sometimes from the same poles. Neither did a very good nor dependable job and the City Council members grew very frustrated—along with grousing residents.

In February 1894, Seymour Price and partner Joseph G. Frakes purchased the gas company and formed a single entity called the Oklahoma Gas and Electric Company. They planned to consolidate gas and electric efforts into a more efficient—and hopefully more dependable—entity.

That didn't work, either.

As soon as the first company started up, the electric power plant burned down. By 1896, Price threw in the towel, handing over control to George W. Wheeler. The company limped along, providing sporadic electric service and no gas service for several forbidding years. Cash was tight, investments were paltry, and to save money, streetlights were turned out during nights when the full moon shined brightly.

A New Century is Born—in Dim Light

Just as the iffy electric and gas service looked the grimmest, things deteriorated even more. Wheeler battled with other investors, chief among them Edward H. Cooke. The resulting argument sucked what little money was left into the ensuing legal skirmishes, leaving the Oklahoma City electric service customers in the cold and dark—literally.

In 1899, the first Oklahoma Gas and Electric Company dissolved without so much as a whimper. Amazingly, Wheeler and Cooke settled their disputes and together formed a new company—the Oklahoma City Gas, Electric and Power Company—in June 1900.

Just as amazingly, despite the electric needs of ten thousand residents, the power

Rare vintage photo shows a service crew at the entryway to the Noble Street power plant—OG&E's first.

The Day OG&E Was Born

Oklahoma Gas and Electric Company was born on Thursday, February 27, 1902. Edward H. Cooke registered the company's articles of incorporation with the Oklahoma Territory's secretary of state.

American novelist John Steinbeck was born on the same day. He later achieved fame with his novel *The Grapes of Wrath*, which chronicled the tragic but dignified plight of the "Okies," who left their farms in Oklahoma during the 1930s, the result of the Dust Bowl.

company and the city administration could not agree on a franchise contract. This venture, too, failed. Once again, the citizens were left in the dark.

The Second Oklahoma Gas and Electric Company— This One Works

By 1902, Oklahoma City's residents would no longer tolerate the iffy electric power shenanigans of the past decade.

In a display of positive Oklahoma spirit, Wheeler and Cooke came back again for yet another try. This time, with significant financial backing from Colorado utility investor Harry M. Blackmer, they formed another power venture—this time approved by the Oklahoma City Council.

The first non-Indian settlers carved sod huts out of the relentless Oklahoma plains.

On Thursday morning, February 27, 1902, Edward H. Cooke formally registered the newly incorporated name of the Oklahoma Gas and Electric Company (OG&E) with the secretary of state for the Oklahoma Territory. Few residents had high hopes for this venture, either.

Indeed, this company's first few years featured even more squabbles than before. But this Oklahoma Gas and Electric Company took. It has powered a city, state, and region for a century.

Revolving Door Executives

When OG&E's first Board of Directors met on March 1, 1902, they chose familiar Wheeler as the first president of the company. Shareowner Henry W. Rule became vice president, and Wheeler's associate Edward H. Cooke took on the dual roles of secretary and treasurer. Their administration—so filled with hope and optimism—lasted all of one month and one day.

During March, Blackmer completed several arcane legal and financial moves. Working from behind the scenes at the April 2, 1902 Board meeting, Blackmer ousted Wheeler and his team. In a show of personal power, he effectively took control of the new electric power company.

Blackmer installed A. H. Branch, a Denver colleague of his, as the new (second) president. William K. Gillett, a New York banker, became vice president (representing Blackmer's financial connections); Charles B. Ames, Blackmer's attorney, took over as secretary and treasurer. Now the structure of OG&E was settled and the company could finally fulfill its promise to deliver dependable power to customers.

Perhaps.

Unexpected Competition

Branch hardly had time to turn the lights on in his office—and in the city—when the Oklahoma City Council, in a surprise move, authorized a franchise to a competing gas company. In the era before strict government regulation of utilities, this sort of thing could happen—and did to OG&E.

The People's Gas Company was allowed to set up operations and sell gas to customers, as well as provide gas lighting. The result was predictable. Oklahoma City was not big enough for multiple gas and lighting utilities. By October 1902, OG&E was again in financial crisis.

Oklahoma Gas and Electric Company in 1902

When the second Oklahoma Gas and Electric Company was incorporated, few probably thought it would last one hundred years—especially given the dismal track record of the several companies that preceded it dating back to the 1890s. Yet, during the preceding decade, those ancestral firms had amassed an inventory of customers and service (power was generated from a single plant in 1902).

When the current OG&E set out a shingle in 1902, it took over assets that included:

- *89 carbon arc streetlamps*
- *120 carbon arc lamps in businesses*
- *7,000 total incandescent lamps for customers throughout the Oklahoma City service area*
- *200 horsepower worth of combined electric motors connected from clients.*

And for this, at times unreliable electric service, customers were charged:

- *20 cents for 1,000 watt-hours (1 kilowatt) of metered electricity ($3.60 in 2002 dollars)*
- *$2.50 per month flat rate for up to ten sixteen-candle-power lamps ($44.95 in 2002 dollars).*

The Race to Build a New Plant

With Blackmer's financial backing, OG&E started construction of its second power-generating plant. But the unwanted competition—combined with the fact that fully 70 percent of city residents still preferred and used cheaper kerosene lamps—created a cash flow crisis.

On October 25, 1902, the following advertisement appeared in the *Daily Oklahoman*:

> *The Oklahoma Gas and Electric Company desires to notify its consumers in the resident portion of the city that owing to the heavy load on Saturday nights, it will be necessary to cut out the resident portion of the city from lighting time until ten o'clock. This will have to be done from now on until our new Electric Plant is completed which we hope to have in operation by November 15, 1902.*

But the plant did not open in November, or even that year. The reason—there was only $62.67 in the bank. And the situation would only grow dimmer.

A Disaster

Just at the time OG&E management was contending with financial woes, they faced a horrible tragedy. On the night of January 27, 1903, a windstorm blew down an electric service wire in town. Although the company engineer was notified of the event, for some reason he neglected to shut down the power.

continued on page 24

Muskogee linemen in the early 1900s.

How Linemen Worked in 1902

Before the second incarnation of OG&E in 1902, predecessor companies limped along supplying regularly interrupted electric power to a handful of very patient customers.

The manner in which the delivery of electric power developed over the decades has evolved into a highly sophisticated, technologically advanced endeavor. At the turn of the twentieth century however, the supply of power, the connection of various lines, and the administration of the company were considerably more casual.

In 1961, George Steinmeyer researched and wrote "A History of the Oklahoma Gas and Electric Company to the Year 1912," as his thesis for his master of arts degree at the University of Oklahoma. (Steinmeyer's work was later published in *The Chronicles of Oklahoma*, the journal of the Oklahoma Historical Society, in summer 1973.)

Steinmeyer's research detailed OG&E's precursors, and presented the key figures in the company's early history. Steinmeyer interviewed Frank Meyer who worked for the ill-fated Oklahoma City Gas and Electric Company and later as a vice president for OG&E. Meyer described the nature of the work in 1901 and was paraphrased in Steinmeyer's work:

The whole labor force would not make a good present-day [in 1961] line crew. Four men worked in the powerhouse, an engineer and . . . fireman for the day crew, and the same at night; these men worked twelve hours a day, seven days a week.

One man was the combination office force and collector, while the line crew consisted of a lineman and one helper.

The lineman made two dollars and a half for a ten-hour day while Meyer, as the helper, got ten cents an hour.

One man, with a horse, was hired on a piece-work basis to change the carbons in the arc lamps every day. . . .

The lines were strung with number fourteen wire, which is quite small and very light so transportation was not much of a problem. The lineman and his helper would take a roll of wire on their shoulders and their hooks in their hands and walk to the job that was to be done. . . .

Early photo of Oklahoma City.

When a man stepped out of his house to pick up his morning paper, he was electrocuted and killed as he stepped on the still live power line draped across his wet front lawn.

The engineer, Charles Schlosser, faced criminal negligence charges and he and the company plunged into litigation. Even worse, OG&E had an awful public relations nightmare and the personal tragedy of a customer's death on its hands. Given the circumstances, Blackmer, now a member of the Board, fired OG&E President Branch, replacing him with attorney Ames, the third president in OG&E's eighteen-month history.

The twists and turns of corporate intrigue of those years continued for the struggling OG&E. Besides the external threats of unregulated competition and the possible negative outcomes of the ongoing litigation stemming from the electrocution, OG&E faced a dismal financial picture. Incredibly, matters worsened. Within the next year, Ames turned on his mentor and ousted Blackmer. Board members squabbled and lawsuits threatened. The shareowners contemplated financial ruin.

An outsider would calm the waters and set OG&E on a clear path to last an equally incredible one hundred years. ■

From tents to sod huts to frame buildings, the early settlers formed a culture and society out of the harsh landscape. Soon they would demand the comforts of water, gas, and electricity.

Within three years, Oklahoma City's residents built a solid, if ragged, community. This 1892 photo looks north on Broadway.

Left: By the time OG&E began in 1902, Oklahoma City was a metropolis.

Thomas Alva Edison, the Father of Electric Power

Thomas Edison heads up the list of American inventor geniuses. More than any of his colleagues, Edison's name is known throughout the land as the one person whose work made more of a difference in people's everyday lives than any other.

Virtually everyone knows snippets of Edison's life, from his early years as a telegraph operator in Port Huron, Michigan, to his entrepreneurial publication of daily news on passenger trains, through his amazing talent at tinkering and his trademark deafness.

Amidst his legion of inventions, the electric light bulb is the most storied and legendary. Besides lighting the world from the darkness of night, Edison devised the systems to create and deliver electric power to consumers, businesses, governments, and communities alike.

History records Edison as inventing the light bulb in 1879 (after a legendary ten thousand attempts—or so we are led to believe). But Edison knew what he was on to. Even before the light bulb was actually invented and patented, records show that Edison had incorporated the Edison Electric Light Company *the year before he invented the light bulb!* Here was a man who clearly knew what he was doing and saw the potential.

The same year of his invention—1879—Edison also devised improvements in the system of dynamos (electricity-producing machines) to achieve an efficient distribution system for electric power. By 1882, Edison had built his first power-generating system in New York City—the Central Electric Generation Station. He branched out with a similar system in Philadelphia in 1884. With business associates, Edison lent his name (and in return received compensation) to power-generating systems that grew up across the land.

When the earliest attempts to bring electric lights and power to Oklahoma City began in the 1890s, the entrepreneurs were on the cutting edge of an emerging technology. Edison would come to have a remote association with Oklahoma Gas and Electric when the fledgling company would experience yet another in its frequent series of structural crises in the early 1900s.

Despite a few failures, electricity and telephone service were instant hits in Oklahoma City.

Left: OG&E engineer W. R. Molinard drove around downtown in an open touring car.

Below: Oil and natural gas propelled Oklahoma's economy in the early 1900s. OG&E took advantage of plentiful local gas supplies to produce electric power.

"Anyone can melt butter with electricity. Try melting steel—tons of it every day. Electricity or not, that would take an enormous amount of energy. Imagine how glad you would be if someone could make that energy much, much cheaper."

**OGE Energy Corp.
1993 Annual Report**

CHAPTER 3

Breathless Expansion: 1904–1920

Ｆrom the rollicking days of predecessor companies going back to the early 1890s, through the first two years of its current incarnation, OG&E had very tenuous times. Various forces came together in 1904 marking a turning point for the company which would go on to celebrate a centennial in the twenty-first century.

Even as 1904 began, OG&E's leadership team argued over financial issues. Financial backer Harry Blackmer, who had pumped considerable money into the company and had placed hand-picked men in management, was in trouble. Blackmer's borrowed money and notes were coming due. He didn't have the cash. Curiously, one of the people who had loaned him money was OG&E President Charles B. Ames.

Ames, a lawyer, together with another investor, Dennis T. Flynn, discovered a wide range of alleged financial improprieties and promptly ousted their mentor, taking control of OG&E. Ames and Flynn worked furiously to reorganize the company's books, but they knew that only an immediate infusion of cash could save the day—and their investments—and keep the lights on for OG&E's customers.

The two turned to yet another bankroller, the flamboyant J. J. Henry. Henry strode into town bigger than life with a reputation as a dealmaker to match his flashy clothes. His high-pressure promises of cash and influence were so convincing, Ames stepped aside, and on March 15, 1904, Henry became the fourth president of OG&E.

Sadly, this was yet another empty promise. By summer, OG&E's main creditor, the New York partnership of Kessler & Company, stepped in and called a halt to the nonsense. Henry couldn't raise the promised cash, or the influence, despite his "get rich quick" reputation. On September 17, 1904, Henry was sent packing, and Flynn took over as president of OG&E, the fifth in two-and-a-half years.

The Management Merry-Go-Round Ends

Flynn really didn't want to be president of OG&E. He was a lawyer and an investor, not an engineer nor a utility specialist. His main interest was saving the company and not incidentally his (and others')

Dennis T. Flynn, OG&E's fifth president, turned to the Chicago utility management firm of H. M. Byllesby and Company to help stabilize the fledgling company's financial woes.

Facing page: OG&E's first service trucks featured a chain drive, solid rubber tires, a tiller for steering, and an unobstructed forward view.

Oklahoma Gas and Electric Company Salaries in 1911

When OG&E expanded service to adjacent communities, the work force expanded. The salary scale published by the company that year showed the differences in skill valuations:

Monthly Wage	Job
$500.00	General Manager
$291.66	Chief Accountant
$208.33	Second Vice President
$208.33	Chief Engineer
$200.00	Treasurer
$200.00	Auditor
$150.00	Superintendent
$108.00	Engineer
$105.00	Foreman
$100.00	Stenographer
$ 94.00	Lineman
$ 60.00	Ledger Clerk
$ 50.00	Grounds man
$ 50.00	Laborer

investments. But rather than fight with other directors, Flynn immediately set out to put an end to the disagreements and set the company on a solid path for the future.

Decades later, through testimony given in a 1935 hearing conducted by a U.S. Federal Trade Commission in a study of utilities, Flynn spoke candidly about their circumstances in those troubling days in 1904. His words were paraphrased in the subsequent *Summary Report* to the U.S. Senate:

They found themselves, a firm of lawyers, with a public utility on their hands. The company was at that time a small affair, serving only Oklahoma City; the service was poor, the lights went out at frequent intervals. The new owners did not know anything about operating a public utility and Mr. Flynn wished to know what made the lights go out. So he called in his friend, Colonel H. M. Byllesby.

The Man From Chicago

When Thomas Edison structured electric power delivery systems in the 1890s, he formed associations with a number of engineers, bankers, entrepreneurs, and managers who slowly gained expertise not only in the efficient delivery of electric power, but also in the efficient management of the power companies.

Engineer Henry Marison Byllesby was one of Edison's early professional colleagues. Samuel Insull and F. H. Tidnam were two others. Each would play a role in the stabilization of OG&E.

Forty-five-year-old Byllesby, called "The Colonel" by his business associates and friends, had snowballed his early knowledge into very successful operations of utilities across the nation. By 1904, his Chicago-based H. M. Byllesby and Company offered experienced utility management services.

Flynn turned to the portly Byllesby to help save and straighten out the troubled Oklahoma City utility. Byllesby agreed, stepped in, and did save OG&E. But Flynn paid a high price.

A New Path of Stability

On October 6, 1904, Byllesby invested $1 million in OG&E, retired all prior debt, and effectively took control of the company. Flynn relinquished his role as president, and prior president Ames took another turn in the top spot, becoming the sixth company president and the third person to

occupy the office in the year 1904. But with Byllesby's influence, OG&E turned to a more stable operation.

Byllesby immediately began a plant-building program. He installed new power generators and the company began paying a modest dividend to shareowners.

By 1905, the company's business office moved from Broadway Avenue near First Street to larger facilities at 110 North Broadway. Symbolically, the headquarters for OG&E was moved to Chicago.

Byllesby brought more Chicagoans into the picture. Insull and Byllesby crony Arthur S. Huey joined the Board, effectively giving Byllesby full control. Tidnam was brought to OG&E as manager. During the next several years, OG&E management orchestrated an expansion in electric and natural gas distribution while customers enjoyed more dependable energy delivery.

continued on page 34

Above: Once inside the office, OG&E patrons could pay utility bills and inspect the latest gas and electric appliances. Here, the members are ready to serve customers in this 1905 photo.

Facing page, bottom: The General Offices of OG&E in 1908. Standing outside the Broadway Avenue storefront are (left to right): Construction Engineer M. Benson, Vice President and General Manager F. H. Tidnam, and Superintendent H. Nelson.

Interior of the boiler room at the Noble Street power plant in 1909. OG&E used both natural gas and oil to fire boilers.

Below: The growing OG&E service fleet is lined up outside the Noble Street plant.

H. M. Byllesby: OG&E's First Legend

After the financial and leadership problems of the early years, OG&E shareowners and customers alike cheered the arrival of "Colonel" Henry Marison Byllesby in 1904. He became the company's original guiding light and "bigger-than-life" persona.

The Pittsburgh native completed mechanical engineering studies at Western University of Pennsylvania and also at Lehigh University. He went to work for Thomas Edison, spearheading development and operations of Edison's landmark Pearl Street power-generating station in New York City. Called the Central Electric Generation Station of the Edison Electric Illuminating Company, the Pearl Street facility was hailed as the first successful power-generating and distributing operation of its kind, going into service in September 1882.

Henry Byllesby got his start managing Thomas Edison's New York City power plants.

While working for Edison, Byllesby got to know Englishmen Samuel Insull and F. H. Tidnam, both of whom played critical roles in the development and expansion of Edison's electric empire. Insull and Tidnam would later play crucial roles in Byllesby's own electric management empire.

Byllesby would also later work with George Westinghouse, serving as vice president and general manager of the Westinghouse Electric Company. Eventually, Byllesby formed his own series of companies focused on the management of utilities, primarily electric-generating and service companies. Byllesby, a prototypical quiet and reserved engineer, underneath was also an ambitious workaholic.

Earle North was a Byllesby employee for many years, and he provided this personal glimpse of the "Colonel" in an interview conducted by George Steinmeyer in 1961 as quoted in Steinmeyer's *Oklahoma Gas and Electric Company, an Early-Day History:*

At Christmastime I'd go into Chicago to visit my uncle and we'd always have dinner with Mr. Byllesby, over at his house.

He would work—he had what he called his office in the apartment; they were living in an apartment at that time, and he would come out of his office about eleven o'clock—he would be working on Christmas Day.

He would visit from eleven to twelve. We had dinner at twelve and when we got through with that, he would say, "Sorry, but I have a lot of things to do," and back in there he went!

Byllesby was a stereotypical business baron in the heady turn-of-the-twentieth-century days. Bigger and bolder than life, Byllesby displayed the same positive spirit as his employees in Oklahoma. His was the "glass half full," and where others looked and sighed and wondered "why," he usually asked "why not." He provided opportunities for many engineers and management personnel at OG&E. President of OG&E from 1910 until his death, Byllesby died in Chicago on May 1, 1924, at the age of sixty-five.

Henry Byllesby's "Colonel" title came relatively late in life, a result of his brief consulting service as a commissioned officer in the U.S. Signal Corps in World War I and subsequent service as a member of the U.S. Army Reserve Corps.

By 1909, OG&E served outlying customers with residential service and streetlighting.

Quiet Times—At Last

As Oklahoma joined the Union as the forty-sixth state in 1907, OG&E quietly, yet constantly, built its power-generating volume while adapting to the new reporting and regulatory scheme of the fledgling state government. That year, OG&E boasted 3,809 electric power customers, 3,398 gas customers, a well-lighted downtown Oklahoma City, and sixty-four businesses having purchased and installed the latest identification symbol—electric signs.

By 1909, Oklahoma City was twenty years old and held forty-five thousand citizens. To serve them, OG&E opened its new Noble Street power station, supplying electric power through natural gas–fueled steam generators. The company employed 160 people and seemed finally on the way to prosperity. Byllesby still controlled affairs from his Chicago office and Ames ran day-to-day operations as company president.

With the outlook improving, OG&E moved next door into bigger quarters at 112 North Broadway in 1909.

Expansion

In 1910 the company undertook the first of several expansions. That year, Byllesby became the seventh president of OG&E, as former presidents Ames and Flynn decided to step aside of the utility management business. Neither Ames nor Flynn really wanted to run the show. They were attorneys and simply wanted to get a return on their original investment. Flynn signed on with a law firm representing Byllesby's corporate affairs and Ames pursued a judicial career.

OG&E purchased the company's first vehicles in 1910—two cars and one truck—to augment the company's stable of horses. But Byllesby had his eye on a bigger acquisition—El Reno.

The El Reno Gas and Electric Company had attracted the colonel's attention. El Reno was twenty-eight miles west of Oklahoma City and was regional headquarters for the Rock Island Railroad. The deal to acquire the El Reno utility was closed in 1909. The next year, OG&E built an electric distribution system in Britton, located ten miles north of Oklahoma City, that provided power service to the small community. With these acquisitions, OG&E now had 10,360 electric service customers and 9,171 gas clients.

To celebrate the company's coming of age, OG&E installed the city's most elaborate electric sign in 1911—a huge flashing affair, alternating

continued on page 39

A Little Homespun Larceny

During the teens, most OG&E residential customers had meters installed at their homes and would be billed for actual power used. Formerly, when most people used electricity primarily for lighting, residential customers had been charged on a flat-rate basis.

With increased use of the various new appliances, including irons, fans, toasters, vacuum cleaners, and the like, electricity use was up. The company would have a more accurate reading with metered residences. Not all residential customers greeted this transition with glee.

A fairly common myth took hold in the kitchens of Oklahoma City. The meters had been installed inside the homes of the customers, usually on an outside wall in the kitchen. The meter consisted of a metal box with a small window revealing dials with numbers to be read by the meter reader.

The myth came about as rumors claimed a heavy metal object placed on top of the meter would actually slow it down—resulting, presumably, in a lower electric bill. It was, as so many such rumors are, false. However, housewives throughout the OG&E service region took to storing their flatirons on top of the OG&E meter box.

Meter readers would have to wait for a moment until the housewife scurried to remove the irons from on top the meter box, lest she be accused of larceny. Until the meter box misconception worked its way out of popular mythology, meter reading took a lot longer.

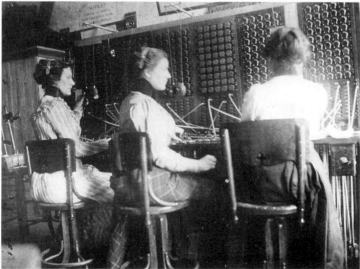

Top: Meter readers, like Robert L. Lankford, drove Model-T Fords. Many meters were once placed inside homes in the early years.

Bottom: OG&E Customer Service consultants in the early days.

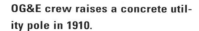
OG&E crew raises a concrete utility pole in 1910.

Above left: OG&E's method of numbering and marking transmission line poles.

Right: F. H. Tidnam, early OG&E engineer, set the company on a solid technical basis. He also kept a scrapbook of photos depicting the company's start-up.

Top: OG&E's fleet of vehicles had grown to include a Model-T Ford by 1913. Shown here are Lee Lash (retired construction superintendent) at the wheel, with crew.

Bottom: This Byllesby-owned Muskogee Gas and Electric Company storefront displays patriotism as the nation entered World War I.

From the September 22, 1920 issue of the Oklahoma Meter

News from the *Oklahoma Meter*

The Main line supplying El Reno with gas was washed out last Wednesday morning at 10:30. When the repairmen reached the break, after rowing more than a mile in a boat, they found the break under five feet of water.

Repair was made and the gas turned on in El Reno at 5:30 Thursday afternoon. A crew of 20 men worked all night under the direction of W. M. Crutcher, Supt. of the Gas Department.

Despite the swift river current, deep water and soft bottom the repair was made in 31 hours—a record in repairs.

The *Oklahoma Meter* began with the September 22, 1920 issue and has continued as a respected and anticipated publication ever since.

In 1911, OG&E headquarters occupied several floors in an insurance building. OG&E signage graced the side and top of the building.

Samuel Insull: Another Chicago Figure in OG&E's Early History

When "Colonel" Henry M. Byllesby took control of Oklahoma Gas and Electric Company in 1904, he installed his longtime Chicago friend and colleague Samuel Insull on the OG&E Board. Insull had a stellar history. He would go on to have a sordid future.

The same age as Byllesby (born in 1859), Insull was born in England and came to the United States in 1881 with the oft-told single-purpose desire to work for Thomas Edison. Persistent to a fault, Insull became Edison's secretary, later moving into management of Edison's large empire of industrial holdings. In those days, Insull came to know Henry Byllesby.

Insull was on the OG&E Board only a short time and left his association with Byllesby in 1907. It seemed to be a mutual agreement. Byllesby's colleague Arthur Huey saw Insull moving into questionable financial practices and convinced Byllesby of the future potential for trouble. The break was a wise one for Byllesby and OG&E.

Huey was supposed to have told Byllesby, "That fellow Insull is going to get us into trouble. . . ." Apparently Byllesby followed the advice, although there is evidence Byllesby and Insull remained friends.

Insull went on to become an influential mover and shaker in Chicago, eventually building a monumental power-generating empire. His office was housed in the huge Civic Opera House, a combination opera performance venue and office building. Insull's relentless drive for power, money, and influence, combined with his divisive toughness, got the better of him and his financial empire collapsed as a result of the Great Depression. Finger pointing and accusations followed him into bankruptcy.

A celebrated international fugitive from justice for several years, Insull was eventually extradited, returned home to the United States, tried, and eventually acquitted on charges of fraud and embezzlement. He died penniless, his reputation ruined in 1938.

between "Oklahoma Gas and Electric" and "Light and Power," commanding 2,160 light bulbs. The garish twentieth century was firmly established in Oklahoma City.

War in Europe; Quiet on the Home Front

During the teens, OG&E consolidated its position as the preeminent electric and gas utility in the State of Oklahoma. The customer base expanded, and more professional approaches to power installation, generation, and distribution were adopted. The company shifted to an expanded motorized fleet of service vehicles, and by the mid-teens, most customers were charged through meters.

With the coming of World War I, especially when the United States entered the war in 1917, OG&E and its leadership team devoted great energy to patriotic service, community activism, and public support of the nation's servicemen and those who aided them.

Byllesby made speeches in tours across the land with nationally known dignitaries. They promoted financial and volunteer support of the war effort. He even accepted a brief commission as a major in the U.S. Army Signal Corps. But with war's end, OG&E returned its full attention to the generation and supply of power to the people of Oklahoma.

In 1917, OG&E purchased the Enid Gas and Electric Company. A quickly expanding power empire in the region flourished and grew in the years to follow.

Return to "Normalcy"

As Oklahoma Gas and Electric Company approached the 1920s, the company had changed enormously. No longer wildly careening from fiscal crisis to managerial infighting to interruptions of power service, OG&E was finally a stable utility. Serving customers reliably and inexpensively was the company's main thrust. The company, its shareowners, and its customers had Byllesby and his engineers and managers to thank for the wonderful transformation to stability.

Few could imagine that as the Roaring Twenties unfolded, neither Byllesby nor his band of loyal managers would be there to lead the company into some of its greatest challenges. ■

Only one meter reader forgot his uniform cap for inspection.

The First Acquisition Outside of Oklahoma City: El Reno

When Henry Byllesby saw that OG&E had become financially stable, he realized the importance of not only growing the company, but also the service region and communities served.

Economies of scale were realized through growth. So in 1909, OG&E purchased the El Reno electric utility and started operations under the name El Reno Gas and Electric Company. (The name was changed to Oklahoma Gas and Electric Company in 1917, as all utilities owned by OG&E were renamed for the parent organization.)

Named for a Civil War hero, Major General Jesse L. Reno, El Reno was twenty-eight miles west of Oklahoma City and was an important regional administrative center for the Rock Island Railroad. In fact, El Reno was another overnight city. When the Rock Island Railroad picked the location for its administrative center in 1889, most residents of nearby Reno City simply upped and moved everything—houses included—to El Reno.

The move even included the three-story Reno City Hotel, which was slowly rolled on logs to the new burgeoning metropolis. Unfortunately, while crossing the Canadian River, the hotel became stranded as its log raft device struck the riverbed. The hotel stayed there—and continued serving its guests—for three weeks until the river water level rose and the hotel could continue its journey to its new hometown.

The first power-generating station in the town dated from 1906 and had changed hands twice before OG&E purchased it three years later.

El Reno had a population of 7,872 people in 1909, and electric service was provided to them, as well as Fort Reno, the Concho Indian School, and the Masonic Orphans Home, all in rural areas away from the community.

El Reno residents have always displayed courage and determination even beyond moving operating hotels across the river. In 1975, the Rock Island Railroad, always the town's major employer, filed for bankruptcy, throwing 950 employees out of work.

In response, El Reno diversified—building an industrial park and attracting a hospital, college, wood products producers, and a publishing company. The community is also home to the OK West Stockyards.

OG&E's first acquisition outside the immediate Oklahoma City area was the electric utility in El Reno, acquired in 1909. El Reno was a regional headquarters for the Rock Island Railroad. Here, OG&E General Manager Jack Owens (far right) is shown with (at far left) D. Van Hecke, Rock Island Railroad division superintendent, and other community dignitaries.

Office members in the insurance building headquarters in April 1919.

Below: George Reed, cashier.

CASHIER NO 1

"One of the most important components in our business strategy is the pursuit of thoughtful, disciplined growth." **OGE Energy Corp. 1999 Annual Report**

CHAPTER 4   # Building and Acquisition: 1920–1930

Following World War I, the nation entered a boom time of contagious optimism. Success turned into excess and the decade of the 1920s ended on a sour note. Through that time, Oklahoma Gas and Electric Company established itself as the main player in power service to the state.

The coming of the 1920s marked a period of power plant building and service expansion for Oklahoma Gas and Electric Company. But expanded power-producing facilities required something Oklahoma City did not have a lot of—water. So Henry Byllesby and his team started the decade by looking for locations to build plants. They had to be adjacent to a good supply of water and able to supply the ever-increasing list of towns and communities served by the growing utility.

Two OG&E members take a break from manhole duty in January 1928.

Facing page: OG&E's local leadership. From left to right: Vice President and General Manager Jack Owens, Information Clerk Catherine Traub, twenty-four-year veteran Harry Nelson, and OG&E Secretary and Treasurer W. R. Emerson.

More People, More Power

In 1922, OG&E began construction of the Riverbank Plant along the Arkansas River near Muskogee, Oklahoma. When completed in 1924, the Muskogee facility brought an additional seventy-five hundred kilowatts of capacity online. It was an enormous amount in those days, but OG&E's customer-base had been constantly growing, keeping pace with the growing population of Oklahoma City.

By 1922, almost one hundred thousand people lived in the city, and OG&E, throughout its several plants and service area, served ninety-two thousand of them.

Changing carbon filaments in streetlamps of the Fort Smith Light and Traction Company was one of the services to OG&E's customers in western Arkansas.

Below: The Fort Smith acquisition came with an electric-powered trolley line.

Expansion to Arkansas

During the mid-1920s, OG&E constantly added service areas, including Shawnee, Ardmore, Ada, Durant, Sapulpa, Holdenville, Seminole, and OG&E's first adjacent-state acquisition in Fort Smith, Arkansas. OG&E would typically purchase the existing electric utility in separate communities and link them to its transmission system.

The Fort Smith region in Arkansas was adjacent to the newly acquired service areas along Oklahoma's eastern border. The acquisition also served Van Buren and several smaller Arkansas communities and even included a streetcar system. Eventually, OG&E would form a power grid extending from central and northwest Oklahoma east into western Arkansas.

The subsequent opening of the Horseshoe Lake Electric Generating Station near Harrah, Oklahoma, showed OG&E's commitment to the future. Construction started on the huge operation in 1923, with the plant coming online the next year. Soon, power requirements would demand several expansions of the facility. OG&E had fully come into its own, a highly respected regional utility.

Then, a double tragedy took place.

Passing of the Old Guard

On Thursday afternoon, May 1, 1924, OG&E office staffers learned of the sudden death of legendary President "Colonel" Byllesby. The sixty-five-year-old electrical utility pioneer died of a heart attack while in his dentist's office in Chicago. Byllesby had been OG&E president for fourteen years, though in reality, he seldom came to Oklahoma City, preferring to tend to his other utility management duties from his Chicago office of the H. M. Byllesby Company. OG&E was typically run by a local general manager.

At the time of Byllesby's death, the local man in charge was James F. "Jack" Owens. Local power service and company operations remained unaffected. There wasn't much surprise either when the Byllesby-run OG&E Board named Vice President Arthur S. Huey as eighth president of Oklahoma Gas and Electric Company.

Huey ran things from Chicago, as well, while Owens tended the office in Oklahoma City on a daily basis. No one was ready for the second shock of the year as Huey died of pneumonia on September 16.

Byllesby had set up a solid structure, and another Byllesby vice president, John J. O'Brien, took over as the ninth OG&E president (and the third to hold the office in 1924). Once again, O'Brien stayed in Chicago, and Owens ran the business locally.

continued on page 47

John J. O'Brien (top) was the last H. M. Byllesby executive to serve as OG&E president from a base in Chicago. Local Vice President and General Manager J. F. Owens ran day-to-day operations in Oklahoma City.

Construction on the Horseshoe Lake Station (left) began in 1923. The completed plant (above), twenty-three miles east of Oklahoma City, came online the next year.

Another OG&E "Bigger-than-Life" Character

When the Arthur S. Huey Memorial Generating Station opened at Belle Isle in 1930, not everyone knew the significance of the namesake, nor the real person behind the honor. Almost no one knows that information today.

Arthur S. Huey was a real-life person, a grand character, and yet another member of the OG&E "hall of fame." Huey first joined the OG&E Board at the invitation of the legendary "Colonel" Henry M. Byllesby in April 1905, shortly after Byllesby came to Oklahoma to straighten out the struggling utility.

Another quintessential American business success story from the age of tycoons, Huey was born in Minneapolis in 1862, where he eventually became a printer and ran a number of theaters.

Long known for his presentation skills, public relations acumen, and boisterous personality, Huey was associated with Thomas Edison's electric-generating interests in Minneapolis. His path crossed Byllesby's regularly, and in 1902, he became vice president of the Chicago-based H. M. Byllesby Company.

Shortly after Byllesby took over management and control of OG&E, Huey came to Oklahoma City, where he became increasingly involved with the utility, eventually stepping into the OG&E president's suite. Huey's expansive ways served both companies well, especially when raising cash for financing or expansion was involved.

George A. Davis, another OG&E former president, believed that Huey was the man most responsible for the development of OG&E. In an interview with Davis conducted in 1961 by George Steinmeyer, Davis gave Huey "credit for having faith in OG&E when the rest of the Chicago people were ready to get rid of 'that bunch in Oklahoma.'" But no one held that extreme view in the Chicago crowd, especially not Huey or Byllesby.

The hefty Huey (estimated as a 275-pounder) was gregarious—and apparently everywhere. Former OG&E President Donald S. Kennedy recalled Huey as having outstanding financial acumen, yet he would spend time tending to housekeeping details. In keeping with his interest in public relations and appearance, Huey could be fastidious about cleanliness.

Steinmeyer quotes Kennedy as recalling a favorite Huey anecdote in 1961:

"Whenever Huey was due in town," [said Kennedy as quoted in Steinmeyer's "A History of the Oklahoma Gas and Electric Company to the Year 1912"], "everyone was put to work cleaning up. On [one] occasion Huey was due in the city in the morning but arrived the night before. Having nothing better to do, he decided to walk down to the generating plant and look around.

"There he found the night engineer polishing brass like a demon. 'What are you doing that for?' Huey asked him.

"The answer was, 'Some S.O.B. named Huey is coming to town and we have to clean things up for him!'"

Arthur Huey died in September 1924, just four months after Byllesby.

Flamboyant Arthur S. Huey served only a few months as OG&E president in 1924.

Experiments and Expansions

In 1925, OG&E began selling home appliances through retail stores. The company hoped to make residential customers more knowledgeable about electric convenience, while at the same time "building the load" of electric service needs.

Officially, the company considered the move a success, but by 1930, OG&E suspended the appliance-selling business in response to a prohibition of such sales by the Oklahoma legislature.

In 1926, OG&E expanded again by purchasing the Chandler Electric Company and the United Power Company, which had provided power to Chandler along with ten other smaller communities in northern Oklahoma. That same year, the Guthrie area joined the fold and a growing complex of interconnected service lines expanded from Enid.

Symbols of Growth

The year 1928 marked the high-water mark for OG&E in the 1920s. That year, OG&E purchased a property in north Oklahoma City called Belle Isle. There, the prior owner, the

Above: OG&E used window displays to promote electric appliances. Here's the latest for 1929.

OG&E Computes Electric Rates for "Wash Day"

The April 13, 1921 edition of the *Oklahoma Meter*, an internal publication of the Oklahoma Gas and Electric Company, proudly announced how inexpensive its power was.

Typically, the heaviest residential demand in the 1920s was "Washing and Ironing Day." So an OG&E engineer computed the actual cost to the consumer in 1921 dollars:

Three 40-watt lights	4 hours	480 watts
Toaster	$1/2$ hour	250 watts
Coffee Percolator	$1/2$ hour	200 watts
Washing Machine	1 hour	186.5 watts
Electric Iron	2 hours	1,200 watts
Electric Fan	6 hours	300 watts

- *Total watts used: 2,616.5 or 2.6 kilowatts*
- *Cost per kilowatt-hour: $0.12*
- *Cost for 2.6 kilowatts: $0.31*
- *10 percent residential discount: $0.03*
- ***Final Cost to Consumer: $0.28***

Twenty-eight cents for the busiest day of the week.

Of course, radios, TVs, VCRs, air conditioners, track lighting, computers, video games, garage door openers, microwave ovens, CD and DVD players, floor sanders, clothes dryers, and the like were a bit down the road.

The architect envisioned the OG&E headquarters with twelve stories. Six would be built in 1927–1928. The following six would wait until 1958 for completion.

Facing page: Construction on the OG&E headquarters and general office building.

Oklahoma Railway Company, had built a power-generating plant to serve its electric streetcar and interurban rail system. Now, OG&E began powering streetcars as well. On the property, OG&E started one of the company's most ambitious undertakings.

While this was going on, OG&E also purchased the Mississippi Valley Power Company, which provided electric service to communities in neighboring Arkansas. This included Fort Smith, which would become that region's headquarters.

Finally in 1928, OG&E made a bold and strategic move by selling all its gas properties in order to focus solely on electric power production and delivery. Curiously, the Board voted to retain the word *Gas* in the company's name, even though it no longer provided this service, because one could never tell when an opportunity to move back into the gas business would present itself.

To celebrate and mark the dramatic— almost breathtaking—acquisitions and expansion in 1928, OG&E opened its long-awaited six-story office building and company headquarters at Third Street and Harvey Avenue in downtown Oklahoma City.

The Art Deco–style building featured entranceways reminiscent of European Gothic cathedrals, clad in Indiana limestone and Minnesota granite. Guests admired carved Tennessee marblework in the sumptuous lobby appointed with the latest electric lighting fixtures. OG&E's twenty-fifth anniversary publication stated, "Every feature of the new building has been carefully planned to increase the convenience and facility of relations with the public and to provide even closer personal attention to every customer."

The new headquarters would eventually have an additional six stories added in 1958, and would serve for decades, up to the present, as the company's corporate headquarters.

OG&E had come a great, almost unfathomable way from the early days of 1902, when officers worried about making payroll and keeping the lights on while furiously seeking capital and loans to save the shaky utility.

continued on page 50

Enid and the Voracious Amusement Park

The history of OG&E had a famous twist when the Belle Isle property was purchased in 1928. Although no longer functioning when purchased, the land was site of an amusement park which flourished during the nineteen teens and twenties.

But the Belle Isle amusement park wasn't the only one in OG&E's past. An amusement park in Enid is probably the reason why OG&E eventually came to supply power to that community.

Enid was part of the Cherokee Outlet during the days before Oklahoma statehood. In 1893, the land was opened for homesteaders and another in Oklahoma's tradition of "runs" took place. Settlers cascaded in carts and wagons lurching from side-to-side in a mad dash to property ownership.

As the community of Enid formed, electric service did not immediately follow. At the turn of the century, Enid was an outpost of kerosene lamps.

One entrepreneur decided that what Enid's residents needed the most was an amusement park to take their minds off the very difficult work in taming the land.

The Parker Amusement Company set up what really amounted to a carnival for Enid. Problem was—no electric service. So Parker built a rudimentary electric system to illuminate the midway and operate the rides. Parker even branched out, selling electric power to neighboring homes.

But the venture didn't last. Operating an electric utility was not like running a carnival. The park shut down and the power generator changed hands a few times. To the rescue in 1902 came a familiar name, H. M. Byllesby. Byllesby bought the power supply and formed the Enid Electric and Gas Company (EE&GC), which immediately built a new plant and increased power output.

For a short time, EE&GC supplied power to Enid's streetcars. A brief and embarrassing controversy erupted about "dips" in power somehow related to the streetcar line demand. The dips caused the cars to lurch and lights to dim in the houses.

Customers worried that such power variances would increase their bills. Although that was not the case, it took the company years to convince them otherwise, even after stable service was ensured.

In 1917, Byllesby consolidated EE&GC with OG&E, which eventually became full owner of the utility.

Elevator operators ready to serve as the OG&E building opened in 1928.

Entering the 1930s

When the 1930s dawned, people held their breaths following the stock market panic of October 1929. Many banks had already shown the effects and an imminent downturn in the economy, with its expected layoffs, was about to begin.

In every way, OG&E was at the top of its game. In 1930, OG&E had more than five thousand miles of power transmission and distribution lines, providing retail service to 192 cities and towns and wholesale service to 42 additional communities.

The 1920s-bred expansions prepared the company well for the future. The customers could depend on a sufficient power supply. And, if there were an unexpected economic downturn, OG&E would have financial reserves.

Changing Titles

For years, OG&E did not have a local president. In 1931 that changed. On May 13, 1931, O'Brien, who had served as OG&E president since the deaths of Byllesby and Huey in 1924, relinquished the title to

continued on page 53

OG&E Employees "Information" Book

Those people lucky enough to become employees of Oklahoma Gas and Electric (indeed, most people consider a job at OG&E quite a respectable one) were given a small booklet to study.

Called *Information for Members of Oklahoma Gas and Electric Company*, the booklet provided a brief explanation of the company's purpose, history. and mission.

The book also included guidelines for work habits and behaviors. The 1929 edition of *Information* provides an insight into expected norms of the day, as well as the emerging concept of total customer service.

"When you see an officer or head of department busy, either with dictation or consultation, do not interrupt him except in emergency. Instead of standing beside his desk and distracting him from his work, wait for a more opportune time or send him a memorandum."

"It is preferable to use the words 'we' instead of 'I' in cases other than those of a strictly personal nature, as 'We will install your meter today,' and not 'I will install your meter today.'"

"Avoid using the word 'busy' when responding to a call which cannot be attended at once."

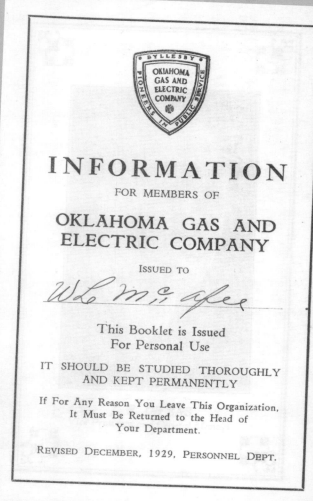

"The word 'flat' as applied to an apartment house, is not pleasing, and you will substitute the word 'apartment.'"

"You must have patience in serving customers; see that every customer in every transaction is treated in a manner indicating that the immediate transaction is the chief point of interest in your mind at that time."

OG&E Life Saving Specialists
ca. 1928

In 1928, OG&E sponsored two resuscitation teams. Trained for assistance within the company, the teams regularly made public appearances and demonstrations, mostly to schoolchildren. Their efforts saved at least one child's life.

A youngster at a picnic fell into a lake and was unconscious when pulled from the water. Two other children restored his breathing using artificial resuscitation. The children later told adults that they'd learned the skill the day before during a demonstration at their school by the OG&E resuscitation teams.

Left: These women wore satin shorts because they gave demonstrations on life-saving techniques using the prone-pressure method of artificial resuscitation (then known as "artificial respiration"). This job often required them to lie flat on the floor, something that shouldn't be done in street clothes. In 1927, the two teams made twenty-three public appearances, mostly to schoolchildren.

Right: This early 1920s parade float shows OG&E's participation in community events.

OG&E members in their spacious new offices. One had to be careful not to knock over the occasional spittoon.

Owens, who was still serving as general manager. With Owens now OG&E's tenth president, home rule returned to Oklahoma City.

Not that it made that much difference. Owens had the ability and won a nice bump in his paycheck. But in reality, Owens had been running the show in Oklahoma City for years. He—and the people of Oklahoma City—really got what they deserved.

But the change marked a turning point not seen clearly at the time. OG&E was now a major player in the power generation and distribution scene, with a positive national reputation. At the same time, the lights in the Byllesby empire were beginning to dim.

The Great Depression would soon cast its gloom over the nation. Slowly, conditions deteriorated. Strong will and hard work were needed to make it through the days to follow. ■

This window display in OG&E's Oklahoma City office announced the beginning of an appliance sales department in 1925. By 1930, appliance dealers had sprung up throughout the OG&E service area and the company eventually discontinued appliance sales.

Facing page: By 1921, OG&E's Oklahoma City vehicle fleet had grown considerably.

From the June 1, 1921 issue of the *Oklahoma Meter*

Special Commendation

John Bell and B. Creveling have been "cited" for conspicuous and noteworthy action in connection with repairs made on the Norman protective switches during last Thursday night's storm.

These two members of the Electric Dept. worked on the substation protective installation during the height of the storm, while lightning played about them.

They displayed an utter disregard for personal safety and comfort, to the end that service might be maintained and the OG&E reputation for efficiency of operation might not suffer.

Hardly a day passes but some member of the Operating Dept. performs an act outside of the strict line of duty, entirely worthy of special commendation, but the work of Mr. Bell and Mr. Creveling was done under such unusual conditions, that a special mention is deserved.

The tradition flourishes today as OG&E members provide heroic service during emergencies of all kinds.

OG&E's Oklahoma City Meter Reader Corps in 1921. From left to right: R. Tyndall, L. Cornett, Relan Clark, J. Minton, E. Lash, W. McCollum, Fred Cunningham, Jack Herlihy, J. Cornelius, J. Quinn, and E. Walker.

OG&E well-worn Ford ready for emergency service in 1925.

Three OG&E members pose in front of Kiefer High School prior to a December 10, 1923 "Electric Show" demonstrating appliances and uses of electric power.

Minority Presence at OG&E

From the company's start, OG&E reflected the Oklahoma and western Arkansas population in its work force.

Oklahoma in Territorial days was a haven for people of many backgrounds. Native Americans from dozens of tribal nations were already here because of the original establishment of Oklahoma as Indian Territory. After statehood, the many descendants of Native Americans stayed and continue to be part of the ethnic landscape. So, too, freed slaves came to Oklahoma, especially after the Civil War, and made new homes and lives for themselves.

The earliest photos of OG&E work crews show an African-American presence—especially in plant jobs as well as in the very hard work of digging holes and raising utility poles. African-Americans attended annual OG&E picnics—separate from their white colleagues, reflecting the social attitudes of the time. But they enthusiastically supported the events.

Over time, the dismantling of barriers brought all OG&E members into a full measure of opportunity throughout the company as well as in society.

In the early days, African-American OG&E members held separate picnics reflecting the nature of the times. Here, OG&E members and their families pose for a portrait in 1929.

Right: Some African-American OG&E workers are shown in this early days photo taken in Fort Smith.

Decorating its headquarters building with lights in 1928 was one of the ways OG&E observed the holiday season.

From the November 28, 1924 issue of the *Oklahoma Meter*

O.G.&E. Adopts a Brand New Service Emblem

Service! Honest service!
Satisfactory, dependable service!
Economical service, rendered with pleasing courtesy.

These are the things we want this emblem to mean to YOU, whenever and wherever you see it.

It was designed in Oklahoma by members of O.G.&E. who honestly believe that your friendship and good will are the greatest single assets our organization can possess—public servants who are conscientious in their efforts to merit the privilege of serving YOU.

It will, beginning today, be the O.G.&E. Service Emblem. It will be used on all motor equipment, office windows, advertising, generating plants, substations, transmission lines and new construction of the Oklahoma Gas & Electric Company.

"OG&E is a people-oriented Company. We try to help all of our customers benefit from our service."

OGE Energy Corp.
1983 Annual Report

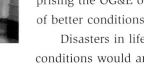

CHAPTER 5

Courteous, Personal Attention: 1930–1945

When OG&E began in 1902, the company set out to provide electric and gas service to customers and make money for the investors. By the 1930s, the company's main drive was to keep the high quality of service streaming to the customers with courtesy, dignity, and individual attention.

OG&E's interest and attention to outstanding customer service dates from as far back as 1916. Certainly, both OG&E President Henry M. Byllesby and Vice President Arthur S. Huey promoted customer attention. By the time of the economic disaster of the 1930s, those companies that did everything they could to keep their customers had a better chance of survival in a time of record bankruptcies.

OG&E survived. One important reason was this growing interest in customer service. The motto during those years was "Courteous, Personal Attention to Every Customer." From these days, employees of OG&E were called "members" instead of workers or employees. The underlying meaning gave importance to everyone in the organization in their mission to serve customers as best as possible.

Facing page: Elegant electric lamps were the rage in the 1920s as shown in this OG&E office window display.

Below: OG&E members assist customers at cashier windows in the headquarters building. Cashier windows were closed at Corporate Headquarters in 1995.

Customer Rates Continue to Decrease

Oklahoma Gas and Electric kept customers during the early 1930s with quality service—and rate reductions. As plants became more efficient, the cost of service to residential and commercial customers continued to drop.

Still, given the Depression's effects, expansion was a thing of the past. OG&E saw revenues shrink from $12.1 million in 1928 to $10.8 million in 1932.

In his 1932 New Year's message to members, OG&E President Jack Owens said, "I am deeply gratified with the manner in which you have responded and met every situation. The loyalty and perseverance of the splendid men and women comprising the OG&E organization will do much to speed the return of better conditions which are sure to come. . . ."

Disasters in life often come in multiples. Before better conditions would arrive, Oklahoma City was inundated with a

The June 15, 1932 edition of OG&E's *Oklahoma Meter* featured vignettes of the massive June 3 flood that devastated much of the OG&E service area.

Few could imagine the tremendous staying power of the service lines as described in this passage:

"One house in the lowlands was washed off its foundations and turned bottom side up. The two service wires were all that prevented it from going down the creek. And the lights [in the house] were [still] on!"

flash flood of great proportions during the middle of the night on Friday, June 3, 1932. The North Canadian River cascaded a wall of water beyond its banks, killing seven people and flooding the entire downtown area of Oklahoma City. OG&E's electric power plants were not spared, and heroic members stood in water and mud while working on high-voltage equipment and lines.

OG&E members helping customers and citizens in emergency situations is part of the job. Stories of heroism and selflessness abound in OG&E history, as numerous floods, tornadoes, and blizzards demonstrate the character of the company time and again. (Such dedication would continue as a company tradition—especially during horrifying events in the 1990s and early 2000s.)

Stabilization and New Ventures

OG&E displayed a hearty dose of optimism during a 1934 advertising campaign to convince residential and commercial customers of the benefits of air conditioning. Citing reductions in hay fever symptoms and getting a peaceful night's sleep, the advertisements provided effective motivation against the muggy heat typical in this part of the country.

Few residential consumers could afford air conditioning units or the increased electric demands it brought along. But commercial customers

continued on page 65

Right: Few residents could afford air conditioning in the 1930s, a situation that changed dramatically years later.

A left front view of OG&E's 1937 model six-man cab line truck. A water cooler and paper cup holder were among its features.

A 1937 OG&E line truck with half-top.

OG&E Legend of Stability–James F. Owens

The early history of OG&E was fraught with rapid changes in executives, which ended when the H. M. Byllesby Company of Chicago took control in the early years. But that period was clouded by leadership from afar—the OG&E presidents were usually headquartered in the Chicago Byllesby offices.

J. F. "Jack" Owens served a lengthy term as OG&E president. He first came aboard in Muskogee in 1910.

However, when OG&E Vice President and General Manager James F. Owens was named president in 1931, it marked a shift to local direct management of the Oklahoma utility. For the next eleven years, Owens ran the show as his own man, even as the influence of the Byllesby name would dissipate and dissolve, a victim of the Great Depression.

In the late 1800s, Owens left his hometown of Aurora, Illinois, at age seventeen to become a school-teacher at Jefferson School in Iola, Kansas. Soon, Owens was promoted to principal. Owens, tired of school and in quick succession, took a job as a newspaper reporter, then several posts as manager of local gas companies in Kansas. Owens liked management work and was hired in 1910 as superintendent at the Muskogee Gas and Electric Company.

During the next few years, OG&E took over the Muskogee operations, and Owens found himself working for the employer he would stay with until retirement. By 1918, his managerial skills placed him in charge of Oklahoma Gas and Electric Company's facilities as vice president and general manager. He was running the local show, even though the president and chief officers were part of the Byllesby empire far away in the Windy City.

With the president's post, Owens drew about him capable management associates and branched out into public and community affairs, enhancing the public image of OG&E while at the same time contributing to the well-being and philanthropic development of the Oklahoma City area and the entire OG&E service area. As World War II started, Jack Owens stepped aside and turned over the presidency to his chief trusted associate, George Davis, on January 1, 1942.

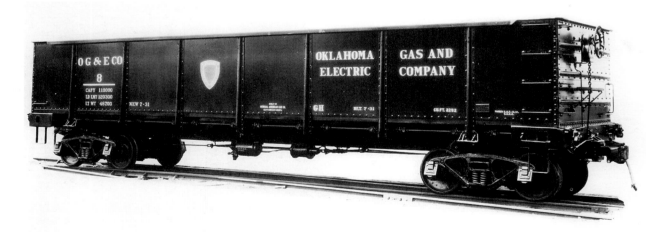

In the 1930s, OG&E had its own set of seventy-ton, flat-bottom gondola cars to bring coal to the Lincoln Beerbower Plant (renamed Osage Station in 1950).

flocked to the phenomenon, resulting in comfortable stores, offices, and theaters acting as a magnet for sweltering residents.

Revenues increased so much that by 1936, OG&E launched another buying venture—this time purchasing the Western Light and Power Company in northwestern Oklahoma. The new system supplied power to Woodward, Shattuck, Wakita, and other communities in this area, becoming an integral part of the company.

In 1936, OG&E adopted a mascot—Reddy Kilowatt.® A whimsical stick figure of lightning bolt arms and legs, a light bulb nose, and outlet ears, Reddy graced publications, outdoor signs, billings, billboards, and advertisements.

A lucky OG&E member sported a Reddy

Kilowatt® costume at special functions, parties, and parades. OG&E even placed a twenty-five-foot-tall electric Reddy Kilowatt® sign on the side of the OG&E headquarters building in Oklahoma City, where it remained for years.

Reddy Kilowatt® continued as an OG&E symbol through the mid-1990s. At the peak of his use, Reddy was used by hundreds of utilities. As the prospect of electric deregulation approached in the 1990s and utilities began creating unique brands, Reddy was discontinued at OG&E—one of the last utilities to do so.

New Storm Clouds

OG&E members spent the late 1930s coping with recovery and dealing with increasing government regulation, and in some cases, outright government ownership of utilities.

A beneficial economic seesaw helped OG&E during the Depression. Although revenue dropped by almost 15 percent, power consumption and the number of customers constantly grew as more and more people, especially in rural areas, came online. By 1939, OG&E revenues had reversed the downward trend and sales rose to $13.6 million.

Top: This lobby display, during World War II, honored OG&E members who served in the Armed Forces.

Inset: Reddy Kilowatt® served as a symbol from 1936 through the mid-1990s.

Lighted OG&E sign displays the Byllesby shield.

The Ardmore Office window display showed the latest appliances in 1930.

But the recovery was marred by a different threat. World War II started in September, and the eventual U.S. involvement placed new demands upon the citizenry—and particular challenges for the electric utility industry.

America was in the midst of back-to-back decades of distraction.

Wartime Limitations and Changes

War brought restrictions on materials. Like many companies, OG&E held off on purchases, expansions, or plant building, instead devoting attention to serving current customers. One of them, Tinker Air Force Base, became one of OG&E's largest customers, often demanding the single largest load throughout the system.

A wartime mark of dedication for OG&E. The numeral three on the white star signified the number of members killed during the war. The numeral 272 on the black star stood for the total number of members who served in the war. The circled eagle represented the 157 veterans employed at OG&E following the war.

Shortly after the United States entered the war following Pearl Harbor, OG&E President Owens decided it was time to step aside and let the next generation cope with the increasing wartime demands.

In January 1942, Owens relinquished the presidency, becoming chairman of the Board. Longtime OG&E (and Byllesby) employee George Ade Davis became the eleventh president of OG&E. Owens, a former schoolteacher, had been with the company since joining as superintendent at Muskogee in 1910.

Owens had brought Davis, a former newspaper reporter, theater manager, and publicist, to OG&E from the parent Byllesby organization in 1920, where he used his public relations expertise in advertising.

A recognized disciplinarian and organizer in the Army during World War I, Davis mustered out with the rank of major. Throughout the war, Davis balanced two jobs—keeping the company operating and assisting in the war effort through his officer's rank as Oklahoma National Guard adjutant general.

Understandably, wartime restrictions curbed any plant expansions, remodeling, or new facility construction. But by the time the war ended in 1945, the pent-up demand for electricity was phenomenal.

Returning servicemen married, started families,

continued on page 69

Advertisements, such as this one in 1942, appeared in newspapers throughout the OG&E service area.

Pull Together **FOR VICTORY!**

OG&E is dedicated to the cause of WINNING THE WAR . . . our power plants are whirling day and night to provide home, farm, factory and store with the same quality electric service they received during normal times.

This is a tough task for 117 of our trained workers already are in the fighting forces and more are preparing to leave . . . the rest will stay and carry on . . . we have no idle minutes, no time for anything but our big job . . . that of being a vital part in the pull to keep FREEDOM RINGING.

OKLAHOMA GAS AND ELECTRIC COMPANY

Major General George Davis, OG&E's Eleventh President

When President James F. Owens called it a career after more than thirty years with OG&E, he turned to a trusted associate to the run the company. He could not have picked anyone with a more varied background than George Ade Davis.

Davis was not an engineer or utility expert. (Neither was Owens, who had been a schoolteacher.) Davis was a public relations and marketing man.

What a colorful past. Davis' first love was the theater. After graduating from Purdue University in Indiana, he took a job as a theater reporter for the *Chicago Journal*, but he quickly moved on into a new role as manager of the famous Studebaker Theatre in Chicago. Moonlighting as advertising director of the *Ziegfield Follies*, a traveling variety show of the era, Davis became a booking manager for New York producers.

But war beckoned. Davis had been in the National Guard since college, and he returned to active duty in 1916, first to handle border skirmishes with Mexico and then right into active service in World War I. During the war, he distinguished himself such that he returned to the United States with the rank of major, and left the Army in 1919.

Davis first took a civilian job as an advertising manager for the Chickering Company, a Chicago-based piano builder. But he was soon lured away by the growing H. M. Byllesby Company to handle advertising and public relations. There, he caught the

eye of OG&E President Owens, who brought him to Oklahoma City as his assistant in February 1920.

For the next decade, Davis worked on public relations with customers. Davis made the motto "Courteous, Personal Attention to Every Customer," work in reality, and within several years, OG&E had assumed a high rank in public esteem. To establish good internal communications and understanding, Davis started, almost as soon as he came aboard in Oklahoma City, a tradition that continues today—*The Oklahoma Meter*—a company magazine. (The *Meter* has been the recipient of numerous prestigious publication awards over the years.)

OG&E rewarded Owens' assistant with the presidency in 1942. Davis' presidency spanned the World War II and postwar years before he retired in 1949. During those years, he handled dual jobs, running OG&E at a time when expansion and plant building were not feasible due to wartime restrictions. He also served as a government advisor, continuing his involvement with the Oklahoma National Guard. In 1946, the National Guard named him major general in recognition of three decades of service to the country.

Following his retirement, Davis remained a member of the OG&E Board of Directors until his death in January 1968.

George A. Davis succeeded Jack Owens as OG&E president in 1942.

Fort Smith, Arkansas office handled
bill payments and offered appliance
displays.

Left: OG&E float in the 1931
Oklahoma City Christmas Parade.

bought homes and cars, and created mushrooming suburbia across the
land. Energy producers and suppliers were forced to expand capacity to
serve the many new homes filled with electric appliances. OG&E met
the challenge, well prepared for postwar prosperity.

Further changes lurked around the corner. ■

OG&E utility poles stand in head-high snowdrifts following a fierce blizzard in Enid in February 1938.

Streetlights illuminate Bethany, Oklahoma, in 1941.

OG&E: Oklahoma Gas and Electric. And Ice!

OG&E was in the home ice production and delivery business in some areas during the early years. It wasn't always by choice, but it was part of the territory. (The ice business came with a number of utilities acquired during the Byllesby years, as several electric companies had ice-producing divisions.)

Home refrigeration was not common in the first decades of the twentieth century and electric home refrigerators were not easily available and affordable until the 1920s.

In prior years, homes had "iceboxes" (a term old-timers continued to use for decades when referring to the refrigerator). Home delivery of ice blocks was a regular business during the horse-and-buggy period, much like milk and newspapers.

OG&E didn't start out as an ice producer, but as

the company grew from 1910 on, it would, from time to time, acquire an electric company that also produced and delivered ice.

It made sense—at least for the smaller firms. Only power-producing companies could afford the refrigeration and freezing unit to make ice in the early twentieth century. It was yet another customer service.

But ice was not OG&E's primary business. By the late 1920s, as increasing numbers of homes installed electric refrigerators, the ice business was no longer profitable. OG&E made two strategic moves in that period. In 1928, gas service to residential consumers was eliminated. And on September 1, 1931, OG&E decided to discontinue ice production.

OG&E delivered ice to customers by horse and buggy until 1931.

"May 3, 1999, marked the start of a tornado outbreak like none ever recorded . . . OG&E Electric Services won a national award for the amazing fast, safe restoration of service to 167,000 customers who lost their electricity."

**OGE Energy Corp.
1999 Annual Report**

CHAPTER 6

The Postwar World: 1945–1960

Few people or organizations were prepared for the wave of returning servicemen who proclaimed their own vision following World War II. They wanted their own homes and their own families in their own communities. For OG&E, the postwar years prompted increased demand, more expansions, another change in leadership, and more devastation by Mother Nature.

OG&E President George Davis shows Vice President of Operations Frank Meyer the proper way to twist wire.

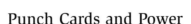

Facing page: About six thousand people came out to this 1957 flag raising ceremony at the Riverbank Generating Station near Muskogee. Its name was later changed to Muskogee in 1972. OG&E's Muskogee and Sooner power plants have been ranked among the top low-cost producers in the nation.

On Wednesday, April 9, 1947, the Oklahoma Panhandle experienced yet another in a parade of windstorms typical of "tornado alley." But this one tested the will of OG&E heroes.

At 8:43 p.m., a monstrous twister took aim at the community of Woodward, obliterating more than two hundred square blocks. The OG&E Woodward Power Plant was right in the path. The plant was demolished, crushing and killing OG&E plant operator Edwin V. Walker and injuring other members.

OG&E members immediately joined together to restore power. They also heroically provided relief and rescue services to hundreds of Woodward residents.

OG&E members delivered portable power generators, emergency sleeping quarters, and food prepared in Oklahoma City. They helped Woodward survive for two days following the massive storm.

Power restoration was important—but secondary. Again, OG&E members put a human face on the tragedy and helped a community.

Punch Cards and Power

In the remaining years of the 1940s, OG&E's President George Davis oversaw the expansion of power-generating capacity and a major step into a modern era.

In 1948, OG&E installed the very first IBM punch card operation. The infantile computer age had not really begun to affect businesses,

The *Meter* in Strange Locations

OG&E President George A. Davis knew the value of communications. When he was brought into the OG&E fold in 1920 by prior President Jack Owens, Davis set out to improve all communications, internal as well as those with the general public. The *Oklahoma Meter* was one of Davis' lasting contributions to the company.

One veteran retiree of OG&E recalled his service in World War II as he was on active duty. He had been working for OG&E and was guaranteed his job back when he returned from the war. Apparently, OG&E members serving their country continued to receive the *Meter.*

During World War II, I was with the U.S. Army Air Corps [later to become the U.S. Air Force]. I was assigned to a special duty where I was attached to the Australian Air Force. I was eventually assigned to a very remote [and secret] location near Darwin, Australia.

For six months, I received no mail at all and had no news of things back in Oklahoma. Not one letter.

After six months in the remote outback, I received my first piece of mail—it was the Meter! *How they found me, I'll never know!*

The 1956 Oklahoma Gas and Electric Company Board of Directors (seated from left to right) are George A. Davis; Donald S. Kennedy, chairman; Howard Henley, secretary; C. E. Loomis; and Carl B. Anderson. Standing (from left to right) are Streeter B. Flynn, Frank J. Meyer, J. W. Westbrook, Marshall Collier, and George D. Key.

but the IBM punch card billing system, complete with the likeness of Reddy Kilowatt,® changed the way customer bills were processed and mailed. It started a new way of life.

By this time, OG&E's customer base had grown to 140,000 accounts, each billed monthly. The automation was warmly welcomed.

The demand for power required more plants. In May 1948, Davis authorized construction of the huge Mustang Power Plant on a 160-acre site ten miles west of Oklahoma City. When Mustang came online in 1950, the plant delivered a monumental 100,000 kilowatts, upping overall OG&E production to 356,000 kilowatts.

By the time the Mustang facility would open, Davis would no longer be running the company. He would turn the five-year, $60 million construction and improvement program over to the next generation of leadership.

Change of Command

In December 1949, Davis retired as OG&E president, turning the leadership over to company veteran Donald

S. Kennedy, who became the twelfth president of OG&E.

Kennedy hired on as an Accounting Department clerk when he was fresh out of college in July 1923. Born the same year OG&E was founded—1902—Kennedy moved to Oklahoma City not knowing a soul, but ended up marrying the daughter of a pioneering Oklahoma family and eventually running the state's premier and most respected utility.

Kennedy had moved through the ranks of accounting and auditing—eventually becoming vice president and treasurer in 1942, the year Davis became president.

Kennedy's detailed and visionary oversight of OG&E's rapid expansion program following World War II made him a natural to take over the company.

More Power

Kennedy was in command when the first Mustang generator started up at 2:17 a.m. on May 5, 1950. OG&E members switched on the 56,000-kilowatt generator without ceremony or fanfare in the middle of the night because engineers were not completely certain it would work properly without taking down other segments of the network.

There was no reason to worry, and the people of Oklahoma started the second half of the twentieth century with power to spare.

OG&E's mid-century expansion included a second Mustang generator expansion of the Horseshoe Lake Station in Harrah from 67,000 kilowatts to 92,000, and an increase in Osage production in Ponca City to 29,000 kilowatts (using a revolutionary hydrogen-cooling system).

OG&E power plants created electricity using steam turbines heated with natural gas or coal as boiler fuel. The idea made sense, because Oklahoma is atop the nation's "gas patch" and supplies were readily available and nearby. Before another generation would come and go, OG&E would use coal as the major fuel to generate electricity.

At mid-twentieth century, OG&E had six major power-generating stations:

- Byng, located near Byng, Oklahoma, built in 1916 and producing 14,500 kilowatts.
- Riverbank Generating Station (renamed Muskogee), dating from 1924 and producing 26,000 kilowatts.
- Horseshoe Lake Generating Station in Harrah, completed in 1924 with 92,300-kilowatt output.
- Osage Generating Station (formerly Lincoln Beerbower), near Ponca City, built in 1929 and producing 46,000 kilowatts.
- Belle Isle Generating Station (formerly Huey) near Oklahoma City, built in 1930 and producing 58,000 kilowatts.
- Mustang Generating Station ten miles west of Oklahoma City,

OG&E on the Cutting Edge

In 1949, OG&E became the first utility in the nation to install a gas turbine generating unit in conjunction with a conventional steam generating unit. Placed at the Belle Isle Generating Station, this combination resulted in substantially increased efficiency.

At the Horseshoe Lake Generating Station in 1963, OG&E built the largest combined-cycle generating unit in the country.

From the July 1954 issue of the *Oklahoma Meter*

4 Years of Double Duty Work is Ended for Norman Graduate

A Norman OG&E man was relieved of the job he held for nearly eight years last month, but started on a new and better job with the company two days later after receiving a degree during commencement exercises at the University of Oklahoma.

Garland C. Council, a lineman with Oklahoma Gas and Electric Co., was promoted to a job in the accounting department of the general office in Oklahoma City after completing requirements for a bachelor's degree in business administration with a major in accounting.

Council, who spent four years in the Air Force during World War II and started to work for OG&E in Norman soon after his discharge, gives part credit for his accomplishment to the company for encouraging him and arranging his working hours around his class schedule.

completed in 1950 and producing 112,000 kilowatts.

After fifty years of operation, OG&E members were proud of the many accomplishments. Still, the biggest and most sweeping changes—and demands—were ahead.

Bigger is Better

Power-hungry Oklahoma kept OG&E on an expansion roll in the mid-1950s. In 1953, an outdoor generator came online near Sulphur, Oklahoma. Renamed the Arbuckle Station, the "open-air" facility produced 78,000 kilowatts.

In 1954, OG&E President Kennedy announced construction of a plant to eclipse the Mustang facility. A new unit at Muskogee Generating Station would give a total generating capacity of 170,000 kilowatts.

The Muskogee operation, when completed in 1956, would take second place as Mustang added a third generator in 1955, upping its capacity to 212,000 kilowatts.

Further additions included a fourth unit at Mustang in 1959 and an eventual sixth power generator at Horseshoe Lake in 1958.

Spurring On the Community

OG&E was now a major player in every sense of the word during the 1950s. The highly respected utility pledged to return the favor by participating more directly in community development.

During the 1950s, OG&E expanded the Industrial Development Department to include community development initiatives. Working together with local Chambers of Commerce and the Bureau of Business Research at the University of Oklahoma, OG&E's Community Development members would work on the grass-roots level.

On the one hand, OG&E would be the catalyst for local communities to determine their needs and develop a plan for the future. On the other hand, as communities considered their eventual goals and strategies to achieve them, they made themselves more attractive to businesses and industries considering relocation.

The end result was increased development of community resources and services, while at the same time providing groundwork for addi-

Fort Smith, Arkansas operating division
building with Reddy Kilowatt® on the
exterior.

tional services for the new business as well as the people who worked
in them. The business benefited, the community grew, and OG&E saw
greater power-marketing opportunities. It was a classic win-win situation and one in which OG&E became a major player.

Community development was a hallmark of Kennedy's presidency.
By the 1960s, it became standard procedure for all senior members of
the company to be active in community affairs at many levels, both
philanthropic and commercial. The company stressed "building the
community." One of the successes of this OG&E initiative was the decision by Uniroyal Tire Company to build a multimillion dollar tire plant
in Ardmore. For Ardmore, the Uniroyal plant was huge—one which
helped build the community into an industrial center. OG&E played a
central role.

continued on page 82

OG&E used billboard advertising to help promote products and services.

OG&E Engineering Manager Ralph Thornton examines ice buildup and damage in Durant following an ice storm in January 1949.

OG&E crew attempts to restore power following a tornado that swept through Drumright in April 1956.

OG&E's Women in the Early Years—Not "Just" Secretaries

OG&E has reflected the times and attitudes of society from the start. But also from the start, the company has encouraged a high level of involvement and participation by women in an industry which had traditionally been a male enclave.

Today's OG&E women can be found in all company endeavors and at all levels. Their predecessors were active and visible even from the early days. Women's participation can be seen from the first issues of the *Oklahoma Meter*. The May 3, 1922 issue described a meeting of the OG&E Club, complete with orchestra performances, officers elections, and planning for the annual summer picnic.

But women's participation was not exclusively social.

Ella Bassett became an OG&E member in 1905 when she was part of the Fort Smith (Arkansas) Light and Traction Company taken over by H. M.

Byllesby. Bassett went on to a lengthy career as an OG&E member, eventually working as an executive secretary with OG&E leadership team members Byllesby, Arthur Huey, and J. J. O'Brien. (She also apparently invested wisely over the years accumulating an enormous amount of OG&E stock.)

In 1924, OG&E members Della Davis and Marjorie Williams of the Bookkeeping Department led a team of men and women members who reviewed and eventually devised a new billing operation for Muskogee.

In the 1930s, OG&E President Owens staged a contest to encourage public speaking among women members. Specifically addressing the growing and troublesome issue of "Government vs. Individual Ownership in Business," the speakers eventually addressed many civic groups throughout Oklahoma and even into neighboring states.

Popular Electric Appliances

Many years elapse between the invention and development of an electric appliance and its eventual adaptation and sale as a useful, affordable purchase.

In May 1956, the *Oklahoma Meter* presented a listing of the years in which these electric appliances were first commercially available for home use (although not necessarily at a fairly reasonable price). Typically, these appliances started out in use at businesses and commercial establishments. Later, through the time-honored process of volume production, they would be available to residential users at more reasonable prices:

1892	Electric Iron		1922	Electric Food Mixer
1901	Electric Toaster		1927	Electric Home Radio
1906	Electric Ironing Machine (Mangle)		1928	Adjustable Automatic Iron
1907	Electric Vacuum Cleaner		1930	Licensed Television (but not popularized until 1947)
1910	Electric Range			
1914	Electric Refrigerator		1933	Electric Roaster
1917	Electric Dishwasher		1937	Electric Blanket
1920	Electric Clock		1938	Home Freezer

In 1958, OG&E's Oklahoma City headquarters got its additional six floors, some thirty years after the building was built.

Expansions, Additions, Consolidations

The 1950s was an expansive time for OG&E members. Demand continued to increase while efficiency of production allowed rates to decrease. It was a marvelous time for the electric utility industry.

By the end of 1956, OG&E's customer count had increased to 320,000—each of whom was using double the electricity they used just two decades before and paying less for it!

As a sign of the times, OG&E built a new office complex at the Arkansas Division headquarters in Fort Smith. When the modern facility opened in fall 1957, it sported OG&E's first drive-up payment window.

In the backdrop of these developments, OG&E quietly participated in a consortium with other utilities to determine the applicability of building a nuclear plant for electric power generation. Fifteen companies studied the possibilities for a four-year period. OG&E opted out of nuclear power generation—much to the company's benefit in later years.

An Enlarged Headquarters

To assist in providing support services in the rapidly growing company, the OG&E Board approved in 1957 construction of six additional floors, doubling the size of the OG&E headquarters building at Third

continued on page 86

The late 1940s saw an upturn in the number of accidents, so the company formed a highly structured safety education campaign. The poster shown below was used in the campaign.

Clubs and Organizations

Over the decades, OG&E has encouraged members to participate in various clubs and organizations. Some have lasted for decades. Others have come and gone with the fashion and interest of the era.

In addition to the social, self-help, and educational activities of the various OG&E clubs, the groups provide opportunities for annual awards and recognitions of member accomplishments.

Annual Service Awards are given to members who have completed five years of service with the company, or multiples of five years. The Service Awards are presented at the company's annual Service Award Banquets held throughout the company.

Above: The OG&E Club Orchestra in 1921. The group played for OG&E Club meetings and dances as well as for local civic organizations.

Right: Oklahoma Gas and Electric Company Girls' Quartette in 1926.

Annual Lineman's Expos place OG&E teams in competition to quickly and efficiently demonstrate their fieldwork expertise in front of their colleagues. Prizes are offered to the most successful teams and individuals in this strenuous and demanding demonstration.

Trailblazers are OG&E members who have completed twenty-five years or more with the company. Trailblazer Awards are given at an annual meeting to "honor those who have served loyally and well for more than a quarter of a century."

The Pioneer Club keeps retired OG&E members in contact with their friends and coworkers "to foster among them a continuing fellowship and spirit of mutual helpfulness." Pioneer Club members also volunteer for many community service projects and events.

Accident Prevention and Environmental Service Awards recognize and reward individual and group achievements in each of these important fields at an annual convocation.

Annual Christmas parties and picnics are held, and Spelling Bee competitions were introduced in the late 1990s.

Men's and Women's Clubs have a long history at OG&E. Over the years, these groups have met to hear various speakers on important events of the day, and to work together to plan and organize the many volunteer civic and charitable events sponsored and encouraged by the company.

At one time, the OG&E Men's Choral Club as well as the OG&E Orchestra provided entertainment at civic events, even serenading meetings of the OG&E Women's Club.

Above left: OG&E President George Davis is shown at a 1940s Trailblazers meeting.

Below: Members perform during Men's Club meeting in the 1980s.

For several years, J. R. Blackburn, supervisor of employee activities, coordinated many of OG&E's Service Awards banquets.

TWO THINGS

Think and Be Careful

This sign was the 1947 Safety Campaign theme, adapted from the "victory sign" during World War II.

Street and Harvey Avenue in downtown Oklahoma City. The OG&E building quickly became a landmark for the growing community.

Improved Safety

The energy production and delivery business is by its nature a dangerous occupation. Mistakes are often fatal. Over the first half-century of OG&E's existence, the company had its share of accidents. The year 1947 was particularly deadly—the worst in the company's history. As a result, then-president Davis instituted a highly structured accident prevention system.

Expanding upon these heightened safety initiatives, by 1960, OG&E had put into action a detailed employee safety program. Relentless in the application and education of correct and prudent safety practices, OG&E went on to acquire a reputation in accident prevention that ranks among the best in the nation. The second half of 1960 saw not a single recorded accident company-wide, resulting in a record of almost three million "man-hours" without an accident.

A Symbol Falls

OG&E's very first power plant was a fairly unsophisticated affair supplying direct current (DC) to several hundred homes from a small facility on Noble Street. DC was the prevailing method in that era, but as systems expanded, DC electricity was not practical to transmit over long distances. Later, utilities changed to alternating current (AC).

Built in the days when OG&E linemen carried rolls of wiring on their backs and walked to locations to connect new customers, the Noble Street plant still produced power in 1959. Because of the change to AC and dwarfed by the power production capabilities of the new plants OG&E had built in the ensuing years, Noble Street was taken offline in 1959 and dismantled in 1961—"retired" after a half-century of service to OG&E.

The end of the Noble Street era marked the stage for a period of sweeping expansion and change to shake OG&E—and the nation—to its roots. Old conventions on power production and distribution fell and a new supply framework emerged.

The only thing constant was change. OG&E became a very different organization—now no longer part of the Byllesby Company. A new generation of leadership would bring about the company's transformation. Those changes would evolve over the next half of the company's life span. ■

From the August 1945 issue of the *Oklahoma Meter*

Enid Veteran Has Honors, No Scratches

First Lt. Charles Gamble, anti-tank officer of the 38th Infantry, may not consider himself particularly lucky, but in our books anyone who happens to have just left his bed roll before it was riddled, or to have dived into a slit trench with his face still covered with lather as a bullet plowed through his shaving kit, is ultra-lucky.

Then when he leads an action of 160 men against 1,000 SS troopers, holding them off for 10 hours and losing a fourth of his personnel, comes off unscathed, and another time is blown from a second-story window, landing on his back in an area between cross-rifle fire, and escapes unhurt, he must surely lead a charmed life.

Such close shaves afford Charles a big laugh, but many another would find his hair turned white or would have dropped dead of fright then and there.

Previous to his entry in the Army in April 1942, Charles was a member of the Northern Division Accounting Department.

OG&E Advertisements over the Years

OG&E print ads have always been informational, explaining the company's commitments. Mascot Reddy Kilowatt® cautions about dust storms in 1938; electric cooking is touted in 1968; the Home Service Department is explained in 1976; environmental considerations are underscored in 2000, and Convergence is featured in 2001.

Reddy Kilowatt
TELLS
What to do
about
DUST STORMS

Dust storms leave a film deposit on lamp bulbs and the glassware of lighting fixtures. Unless these are washed the lighting efficiency is impaired as much as 30%. This means that you are receiving but two-thirds of the light you are buying.

This friendly help is being sent in keeping with our policy at no time to sell "short weight" electricity. We want you to receive full value for your pennies.

We urge, also, that you consult our Lighting Department regarding ways and means of receiving the maximum illumination at minimum cost. Such consultation will probably save you dollars, in both your home and place of business. This service, of course, is free and without obligation.

OKLAHOMA GAS AND ⊕ ELECTRIC COMPANY

An Oklahoma Institution • Established, Oklahoma Territory, 1902

Good Cooks...
Cook Better Electrically!

...and some ovens even clean themselves ELECTRICALLY!

let electricity do it for you!

With a new electric range you're in complete control of the cooking temperature because they're fully automatic and flameless... and this is why you're automatically a better cook. Day after day, you can rely upon accurately selecting the same, desired cooking temperature and maintaining that temperature as long as you choose. You have the ability, with an electric range, to accurately predict and consistently produce the same marvelous results day after day.

$25 CASH INSTALLATION ALLOWANCE WHEN YOU BUY AND INSTALL A NEW FLAMELESS ELECTRIC RANGE DURING APRIL, 1968. FOR OGE CUSTOMERS ONLY. BUILT-IN ELECTRIC RANGES IN NEW HOMES NOT ELIGIBLE.

OG&E ELECTRIC SERVICE

"OG&E's Home Service Department Is An Extra Benefit To You."

"OG&E home service consultants show and tell our customers how to use electricity efficiently. This description covers a lot of different subjects... but the people I talk to want to know about the operation of electrical appliances including heating and air conditioning systems. Plus, they're very interested in knowing what they can do to be more efficient in the amount of electricity they use in the home.

For instance, the subject of my demonstration given to a class at The South Oklahoma City Junior College recently was a familiar one. Insulation. The insulating qualities of any home, old or new, can be improved by installing adequate insulation in attics, sidewalls and floors—including those over crawl spaces. Plus, energy savings are increased by adding storm windows and doors, installing weather-stripping, and caulking around window and door frames.

Proper whole-house insulation does represent the most significant opportunity our customers have to save on the amount of energy needed to heat and cool a home."

Providing you with information on the proper use and benefits of electricity is a service OG&E offers you through its home service department. This service will be available today and... in the future that looks electric.

YOUR FUTURE LOOKS ELECTRIC

OG&E ELECTRIC SERVICE

Efficiency Tip
Positive Energy

• Have OG&E install a free PEAKS device and you'll cut your cooling costs an average of $30 this summer. **OG&E** ELECTRIC SERVICE

ENJOY THE PERKS OF PEAKS.

"For many companies, being green means putting one of those little recycled paper logos on a brochure. But unless you do much more, you haven't lived up to your environmental responsibility."

OGE Energy Corp.
1993 Annual Report

CHAPTER 7

A New Age: 1960–1979

OG&E President Donald Kennedy meets with another president, U.S. President Dwight D. Eisenhower.

Facing page: OG&E President Donald Kennedy at a 1961 groundbreaking ceremony in Shawnee.

OG&E's first half-century was sprinkled with financial and ownership crises, growth, expansion, lower rates, and increased customer attention. The second fifty years would see the foundations of the power industry shaken in unimaginable, dramatic ways.

OG&E expanded the march of technology in the new age dawning of the 1960s. The introduction of computers into many areas of OG&E was one of the first steps. Although OG&E had used an IBM punch card billing system for more than a decade, that unit was not, strictly speaking, a computer. In 1960, after two years of planning and testing, an IBM 1401 computer system began recording customer power usage and simultaneously determining and predicting peak-load demands. For the first time, customers were clearly identified in the computer records down to the pole from which they received their service.

By today's standards, this is not earth-shattering. But in 1960, it marked a technological revolution in the power industry—away from manual recording toward the power of the chip. Few realized then the impact the new technology would have in the ensuing decades.

Power Network

In 1961, OG&E President Donald Kennedy and his leadership team greatly enhanced interconnectivity. OG&E, along with others in the South Central Electric Companies (SCEC), a consortium of eleven investor-owned utilities, entered into an agreement with the Tennessee Valley Authority (TVA) to engage in a "power swap."

The proposed arrangement benefited both partners because TVA experienced peak loads in the winter, while OG&E always had increased demands during the summer air conditioning season. The trend would only get worse as more and more residential customers bought and installed home air conditioners in the 1960s. Increased loads in the summer were real phenomena for OG&E in the 1960s. One retiree relates they could actually predict huge jumps in power demand when Sears or other retailers would advertise air conditioner sales. Residential consumers would buy the sale items, take them home, plug them in,

and immediately double their power demands. It got so that OG&E staffers hoped for prior announcement of Sears' air conditioner sales just to be ready!

To add reliability and create flexibility, OG&E and other power companies built a power grid and transmission line system. Power sharing was born. The result linked investor-owned utilities in Oklahoma, Kansas, Missouri, Arkansas, Texas, Mississippi, and Louisiana. Although expensive, the grid was cheaper than building new plants to supply the anticipated power needs.

Another "Largest"

OG&E still had to build new plants to keep up with general demand despite the power pool arrangement. The grid, for the most part, permitted utilities to purchase or swap power in peak periods. But as Oklahoma continued to grow, so did base power demands for OG&E's customers.

OG&E's Horseshoe Lake Station continued to expand in the 1960s. Top photo shows the plant as Unit No. 7 came online in 1963; bottom photo shows the control room.

In 1966, OG&E began construction on a $30 million, 415,000-kilowatt steam turbine generator at Horseshoe Lake near Harrah, Oklahoma. The installation was the largest built in the state at that time. OG&E built its first Horseshoe Lake unit in 1924 and enlarged capacity several times. When the new unit was fired up in 1969, Horseshoe Lake produced almost one million kilowatts of power.

continued on page 94

OG&E's Company Man, Wayne A. Parker

Wayne Parker had spent virtually his entire working career with OG&E when he was chosen thirteenth president in 1966.

When Parker graduated from Oklahoma City's Central High School in June 1926, the strapping eighteen-year-old looked for work. He found a job as a temporary laborer in OG&E's Construction Department. During his sweaty summer of 1926, Parker found he liked the company—far better than the hard work he was assigned to do in the Construction Department. Years later, Parker would be manager of construction for the entire company.

The following year, Parker enrolled at Oklahoma City University. He continued to work summers and part-time at OG&E to pay the tuition. While at school, Parker became a star on the OCU football team. Later, he completed his studies at the University of Oklahoma where he received a degree in electrical engineering in 1935. Returning to OG&E with his fresh diploma in hand, Parker toiled in the Electric Department as foreman.

Called to active duty during World War II, he was a commissioned officer, eventually distinguishing himself for heroism, receiving the Navy Cross for literally plugging his body into a hole from an enemy shell which had ripped through the engine room of the U.S.S. *Ringgold*. His action stopped the flooding and saved the ship and the men.

Returning to OG&E following the war, Parker started a steady rise in the ranks. In the 1950s, a string of superintendent assignments brought him into close contact with his mentor, Donald Kennedy. He oversaw construction of the huge combined-cycle steam-turbine generator at Horseshoe Lake.

In the mid-1960s, Parker became vice president and assistant to the president. It was an easy step to the president's chair when Kennedy relinquished the presidency in 1966. Following Kennedy's lead, Parker continued with external affairs involvement, taking leadership roles in community and professional organizations. Parker continued as OG&E president until succeeded by James G. Harlow in 1973.

Wayne Parker had served in many jobs throughout OG&E when he took over as president following Donald Kennedy in 1966.

SCEC-TVA:
Eleven Companies Agree to Cooperate

In the spring of 1961, several utilities in Oklahoma, Arkansas, and Mississippi suggested a seasonal interchange of power with the Tennessee Valley Authority (TVA). The idea called for TVA to supply power to the companies in summer and the reverse situation in winter.

When presented with the plan, OG&E's President Donald Kennedy said, "It is a good idea and I wish you the best of luck, but I find it hard to believe that you can get eleven companies to agree with you on anything—even the time of day."

Kennedy's skepticism aside, over the next eight months, representatives from the companies formed a group called the South Central Electric Companies (SCEC). Arduous, intense, and tedious negotiations eventually resulted in a landmark agreement that was approved by the Federal Power Commission. A total of fifteen hundred megawatts was eventually moved between companies in Arkansas, Oklahoma, Mississippi, Louisiana, Texas, Kansas, and Missouri.

The SCEC actually had its roots in the Southwest Power Pool (SWPP). Formed originally upon the urging of the federal government during World War II, SWPP eventually counted fifteen major investor-owned electric utilities. Of the fifteen, eleven participated in SCEC and the SCEC-TVA power interchange.

Mid-Decade Transition

On December 1, 1966, Kennedy, OG&E's twelfth president, relinquished day-to-day management of the company—a role he had held since 1949. Continuing as CEO and chairman of the Board, Kennedy passed the presidency to thirty-four-year OG&E veteran Wayne A. Parker, who became OG&E's thirteenth president.

Parker had come up through the ranks at OG&E as had Kennedy. Unlike his early-year predecessors, Parker had climbed the poles in ice storms, served as an elevator operator in the headquarters building, and worked in Transmission and Distribution.

The first OG&E president to have a degree in electrical engineering, Parker was the ultimate company product. His knowledge of the company operations and facilities, combined with his understanding of the industry, would serve the company well.

The Seminole Plant

One of Parker's first jobs was to supervise the design and construction of the new Seminole Generating Station to be built on a lake east of the Oklahoma community of Konawa.

By the late 1960s, all of OG&E's generating

Guests at Lake Konawa were greeted with this signage featuring Reddy Kilowatt. OG&E built the 1,350-acre Lake Konawa for cooling the Seminole units and then opened the lake for picnicking, boating, fishing, and swimming as a public recreation area.

plants used natural gas as the primary
fuel to power the steam turbines. The
plants at Arbuckle, Byng, the remaining
Belle Isle facility, Enid, Horseshoe Lake,
Mustang, Osage, Riverbank, and
Woodward-Shattuck all relied upon this
fuel source so integral to Oklahoma.

The $45 million Seminole facility
was to generate about 550,000 kilowatts
when online. To further enhance the area, OG&E expanded the cooling
reservoir, creating the 1,350-acre Lake Konawa, which was subsequently
opened for public recreation. The dual-land-use theme won praise from
residents, providing fishing, swimming, and boating. Two additional
power-generating units would be added at Seminole, increasing the
plant's total output to more than 1.6 million kilowatts.

OG&E's vehicle fleet continued to
modernize and expand through
the 1960s.

Streamlining and a Quiet Decision

In 1971, OG&E worked out an arrangement to eliminate some of the
overlapping territorial services with other regional power producers and
suppliers.

That year, Public Service Company of Oklahoma (PSO) "swapped"

Two OG&E members reflect
Cold-War tensions of the 1960s
as they conduct a Civil Defense
radiation check.

several communities with OG&E. OG&E started serving Mustang and Union City, while OG&E turned over Jenks to PSO. OG&E also acquired fifty-seven sections of rural area from PSO, while handing over another twenty-four sections in the Jenks area to PSO.

In 1972, OG&E management mapped out a plan to expand the power-generating capabilities at the Riverbank Plant. Renamed the Muskogee Generating Plant, two new 515-megawatt generators were installed. They would be fired by low-sulfur Wyoming coal, marking a significant departure from the total reliance on Oklahoma natural gas.

No one, not even the most inspired visionary OG&E leader, imagined in 1972 how events would transform the way the nation and the world would look at energy within just a few years. What seemed to be an experiment to save money generating power turned out to be the salvation of the company—especially during years of scarce, expensive, and politically sensitive natural gas and oil supplies. When the famous Organization of Petroleum Exporting Countries (OPEC) oil crisis of 1973 took the country—and the world—by storm, OG&E would be run by different leadership guiding the steady hand of coal conversion, propelling the company into the uncertain age.

Serving on the 1976 Board of Directors of the Oklahoma Gas and Electric Company (standing from left to right) are William Little Jr., Carl Anderson, John Griffin, and A. Curtis Goldtrap. Also (seated from left to right) Christine Anthony, Wayne Parker, Robert S. Kerr Jr., Donald Kennedy, Pat Kelley, and Jim Harlow.

Another New Leader

James G. "Jim" Harlow Jr., an Oklahoma native like his predecessor Parker, graduated from the University of Oklahoma. The young Harlow spent two years as an officer in the U.S. Navy. Studious and determined, Harlow joined OG&E in 1961 as a research analyst. Like prior OG&E President Kennedy, Harlow's specialty was accounting.

Harlow set out to learn everything he could about OG&E in order to find more efficient and effective ways to do business and help customers. He quickly moved through the organization's hierarchy, becoming assistant treasurer in 1966, treasurer in 1968, and corporate secretary and treasurer the following year.

In 1973, Parker stepped down as president, capping a forty-plus-year career with the only company he ever worked for full time. The "company man" Parker turned over the responsibilities of day-to-day operations to Harlow, who became OG&E's fourteenth president. Neither man knew at the time that Harlow would be the man in charge during some

Service truck in 1978.

James G. Harlow Jr. became the fourteenth president of OG&E in 1973.

By the late 1970s, many OG&E customers had installed electric heating and cooling units in their homes sparking an increase in electricity demand.

of OG&E's most challenging days. Adversity began almost immediately.

A Crisis in Energy

The energy world changed briskly in 1973. It started when OPEC, the Organization of Petroleum Exporting Countries, enacted an embargo on exported oil to importing countries.

The United States had gone from self-sufficiency in oil production and refining to importing a significant portion of its needs. American consumers were caught in a supply-and-demand crunch. The price of oil and gasoline skyrocketed as supplies dwindled. Television news programs started many broadcasts with film of long lines at gas pumps.

Gasoline is but one component produced from crude oil—imported or domestic. Heating oil is another. Electric utilities on both the East and West Coasts of the United States relied much more heavily on heating oil as the power source for electric generation. The embargo had an immediate effect upon the price and availability of the utilities' oil supplies—and those utilities virtually overnight sought dramatic rate increases. As quickly as that, the era of constantly lower electric rates ended.

Through wise choices by OG&E leadership and the happy location on top of the fabled "gas patch," OG&E did not immediately feel this crunch. OG&E's power plants overwhelmingly used lower-cost natural gas to supply energy to its turbines. That, too, would change.

Supply and Demand

Few economic events happen in a vacuum. As supply-and-demand drove up the cost of all interrelated energy production, eventually, OG&E saw the price of natural gas supplies increase as well.

To cope with the new and changing world of energy, Harlow and his management team increased construction on plant production in 1974 and 1975. But the need to build more power plants combined with the ever-increasing costs of generating fuels had its effect upon OG&E. In 1975, after a summer of record power consumption by OG&E customers (a record peak of 3,185,000 kilowatts was achieved in September of that year), OG&E was forced to apply for its first rate increase since 1954.

"We Will Not Build the Nuclear Plant."

In February 1995, two months before his death, former OG&E President Donald Kennedy lunched with former OG&E Senior Vice President Ross E. Harlan. Harlan asked Kennedy what he thought was his most important decision.

Kennedy replied, "The decision in the late 1960s to cancel the plans for building a nuclear power plant." Kennedy recalled that a consulting firm had presented a report recommending a nuclear plant be located in a wooded area between McAlester and Ada, Oklahoma.

An environmental impact study and other reports had been filed. At a scheduled "go-ahead" meeting of the consultants, OG&E leadership, and engineering and power production personnel, final reports and recommendations were presented. After the reports were given, Kennedy asked if there were any further comments. There being none, he promptly and decisively stated, "We will not build the nuclear plant." Then, to a stunned and silent audience, he nodded and immediately left the room.

Subsequent events proved the wisdom of Kennedy's decision.

OG&E moved into a period of constant plant expansion and the need to use more coal in power production. Federal government regulation dictated conservation measures and pollution controls. Simple economics forced OG&E to increase rates charged to customers—itself a complex process because of government regulation.

The electric industry had entered a new era: one of ill will among regulators, suppliers, and customers.

A Decision Proves Correct

Through happy circumstance, OG&E was ahead of the issue during the crisis years. The company had decided not to pursue nuclear energy. In the late 1960s, the company commissioned an independent consultant's study of power-generating fuel supplies for OG&E's future. The findings—and recommendations—were as surprising as they were counterintuitive. Although OG&E had easy access to natural gas, the study recommended a strategic move to switch away from that local power source.

The power source in OG&E's future would be the power source of the past—coal. The nearest good-quality, clean-burning, low-sulfur coal would come from one thousand miles away in Wyoming. Soon, OG&E had two coal-generating power units in operation as a test and serving as the vanguard of strategic change for the company.

The timing could not have been more exquisite.

Expanding and Financing the Venture

OG&E's 1975 marketing theme was "Dawn of a New Energy Era," and the choice was clear. OG&E would expand coal-fired power production. In April of that year, OG&E purchased 10,500 acres of land south of Ponca City, Oklahoma, for the construction of a new coal-fired facility to be called the Sooner Generating Station. By 1980, OG&E had four coal-powered generators, two at Muskogee and two at the new Sooner plant. By then, almost half the power output was from coal-fired generating equipment.

continued on page 102

Coal pile at the Muskogee Power Plant. OG&E added clean-burning Wyoming coal to its fuel mix of electric power production as a means to counter energy concerns of the 1970s.

The "Live Better Electrically" sign was removed from the OG&E headquarters building in 1978.

Coal train heads back to Wyoming's Powder River Basin after delivering coal in Oklahoma.

During 1976, OG&E received smaller-than-requested rate increases from state utility regulators. With the increases now not covering expenses, OG&E went into debt to finance expansion of facilities and to manage day-to-day operating expenses. This financial shift in the company's balance sheet persisted for several years to come.

Even amidst these woes, the future was taking shape as in July 1976, the first Muskogee coal-fired power-generating turbine came online. It marked OG&E's first use of coal as a main generating fuel since the late 1930s.

The Increasing Pace of Change

In the late 1970s, OG&E noted an overall increase in winter power usage. Winter typically saw lower demand because summer air conditioning usually created peak demand days. But now, power use was going up year-round because many OG&E customers had switched to or installed electric heating units in their homes. Because winters in the area are a bit less severe than in the northern states, electric heating was seen as a clean alternative to coal, natural gas, or oil for home heating.

The increased customer power demand coupled with the added demands of plant expansion created more administrative duties. To streamline operations, OG&E acquired state-of-the-art office technology.

One Addition, One Subtraction

In 1978, the company installed a new computer system for members, creating the "work station" concept of terminals in many locations for employee work and access. It was a small move, but marked a transition in work habits that would be universal by the 1990s.

Also in 1978, the venerable landmark electric sign on the OG&E Oklahoma City headquarters building was taken down. The sign touting "OG&E—Live Better Electrically" had run its course, after beaming its message in various forms since 1911.

To further highlight the pace of change, 1979 marked the first delivery of coal to the new Sooner plant. A Santa Fe locomotive team, pulling 109 coal cars behind it, arrived at the Sooner power plant on the morning of March 22, 1979. Each car carried one hundred tons of low-sulfur, cleaner-burning coal from the Black Thunder Mine, located near Gillette, Wyoming. The plant expected to consume six of the one-hundred-ton carloads per hour, requiring approximately six full trains full of coal every week, or in other words, about a trainload every thirty hours. A new era had begun for the seventy-seven-year-old OG&E.

Yet, even though the company had weathered the multiple crises, more challenges were ahead. Because the world had changed so dramatically in such a short time, the way OG&E operated would require massive organizational change. The days about to unfold would give Jim Harlow some of his most trying times. ▪

"We are doing our part to create change where we see benefit for our customers, our investors, and the communities where we live and work."

OGE Energy Corp.
2000 Annual Report

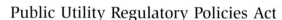

CHAPTER 8   # Change or Perish: 1979–1989

I n less than a decade, OG&E's power production and rate structure, which had for so many years been a source of pride, had turned to deep concern. Mounting costs and their resulting financial pressures were worsened by the prospect of reducing peak demand. The company would need to change in order to prosper in the last decade of the twentieth century.

OG&E's increasing costs were not being met by increasing revenue. The addition of coal-burning power production required expanding the Muskogee and Sooner plants. The cost of fuel to create electric power was increasing and so were power demands by customers. Then, in response to the OPEC oil crisis in the mid-1970s, the federal government had instituted an energy and conservation policy affecting all businesses and industries.

Facing page: Clockwise from top left: Muskogee Linemen Raymond Salee, Harold Parsons, and Johnny Barnett train on live 34,500-kilowatt lines in 1981.

Public Utility Regulatory Policies Act

In November 1978, the United States enacted legislation affecting most facets of energy production, sales, and consumption. The 1978 National Energy Act consisted of five separate and major pieces of legislation: The Energy Tax Act, The Public Utility Regulatory Policies Act, The National Energy Conservation Policy Act, The Power Plant and Industrial Fuel Use Act, and The Natural Gas Policy Act.

The Public Utility Regulatory Policies Act (PURPA) particularly affected publicly owned electric utilities. One provision of the act required electric utilities to purchase power from "qualifying facilities at avoided cost."

In essence, this requirement forced utilities to pay other private power producers for electric power in lieu of building new plants. OG&E, like other utilities, had to purchase power from suppliers, at a price to compensate them for capital investment instead of building a

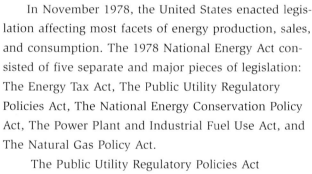

105

A Parade of Acronyms

With the energy and fiscal crises confronting OG&E as the company started the 1980s, the OG&E Marketing and Consumer Relations Department switched into overdrive to deal with the challenges. Like the start of the Franklin Roosevelt administration during the height of the Great Depression in 1933, OG&E participated in a series of programs, all designed to assist consumers with an understanding of their energy needs and consumption, and offering ways to cut back on their demand, especially during peak periods. ECHO, AWARD, ARCS, and PEAKS initiatives all grew out of this imaginative period.

ECHO (Energy Conservation Helps Oklahoma) was introduced in the spring of 1981, and offered home energy audits performed by OG&E under the jurisdiction of the Oklahoma Corporation Commission.

AWARD (Audit and Weatherization Aid Reduce Demand) provided cash incentives to homeowners who requested an ECHO audit, then enacted specific recommendations for energy savings.

ARCS (Arkansas Residential Conservation Service) was a program similar to ECHO offered to the Arkansas residents receiving OG&E service.

PEAKS (Planned Economy and Kilowatt Saver) started in Arkansas and was later applied to Oklahoma. This system used local special thermostats to cycle air-conditioner compressors off for 7 1/2 minutes each hour during periods of peak demands.

These programs proved quite popular and by July 1983, 4,000 Oklahoma and 487 Arkansas customers had received more than $775,000 in AWARD payments.

new plant. This practice limited the utilities' ability to expand to meet their customer needs. The specific restrictions faced by OG&E only exacerbated a particularly difficult time for the company and its members.

Bleak Conditions

Speaking at the 1980 OG&E Annual Company Conference, Jim Harlow had blunt words for his employees: "We are no longer designing an electric system we believe the public needs," Harlow told the team. "We are doing what we can to provide electricity based on the rates that we are allowed. The last rate decision was the one that broke our back."

In light of the financial situation, OG&E was faced with a public relations problem as well. "As prices go up, we may have to develop programs so we don't lose credibility with our customers by the way they are being treated."

It was a stunning turn of events for a company dedicated to customer service. Worse, the U.S. Department of Energy had wheeled out a national energy policy that implemented the Power Plant and Industrial Fuel Use Act of 1978, that required utilities to phase out natural gas use within ten years. What had started as a transition by OG&E to a lower-cost fuel source now was mandated by the federal government, at a pace that was not financially possible given the regulatory rate squeeze. Quite a fix, indeed, for OG&E.

All this was against a backdrop of financial problems. "The present financial condition of the company is bleak," said Drake Keith, OG&E senior vice president, Finance, at the same 1980 conference. "If we get the emergency temporary rate relief we have asked for, it will hopefully slow the continuing rate of financial deterioration of the company."

If that didn't cause OG&E members to take notice, nothing would. Corporate representatives are seldom so candid.

It Starts with Consumer Relations

The first steps in OG&E's institutional change included harkening back to the motto embracing the company's consumers. An information campaign explained the conditions and the reasons for rate increases. Marketing now had consumer relations as its main endeavor.

For decades, company advertising and marketing policy

Word Processors Are Coming!

stressed the convenience of electric appliances and the ever-lower cost of powering them. More power consumption meant a noticeably better life for OG&E's customers—and a better bottom line for OG&E's shareowners. In that era, it was expected and accepted.

Next, the company initiated a load-reduction awareness campaign. OG&E directed Customer Relations to reduce the growth rate of on-peak summer load.

The air conditioning awareness campaign of the mid-1930s, when few residential customers could realistically afford it, had now come full-circle as virtually all residential users had home air conditioning units and were faced with the prospect of insufficient power to run them.

Home insulation, raising thermostats, and residential energy conservation all entered the marketing language in this era. It marked a stark new direction for OG&E. The move came just in time as yet another twist to OG&E's fortunes took place: The summer of 1980 was the hottest in years for Oklahoma and Arkansas.

Belle Isle Retired

The fifty-year-old Belle Isle Station was the first victim of the new era in energy. The age of the plant com-

Belle Isle Station.

bined with the new federal regulations governing natural gas–fired operations pushed the plant into obsolescence. Worse, the cooling lake had become so silted, the facility was literally inoperable.

After 1980, Belle Isle Station was dismantled and the property eventually sold to a developer. It was another transition in an era of change.

Technological Advances

Tough times require tough people—and tough companies. In this period of cash crunch, OG&E never stopped looking toward technology as a means to contribute to overall cost-savings.

In 1983, eight decades of traditional meter reading came to an end. The 116 OG&E meter readers now carried "Roadrunner" devices, which electronically recorded and transmitted data to the OG&E central computer each day.

To relieve storm-related power outages, OG&E invested in a fleet of "mobile substations." The mobile units also did double and triple duty when used during planned or preventive maintenance, construction, or rehabilitation of any of the 650 OG&E freestanding substations in use during the 1980s.

Poteau Meter Reader Reba Tamplin records data manually. Electronic devices came to OG&E in 1983.

In 1983, Donald Kennedy decided it was a good time to step down as chairman of the Board of Directors. In Kennedy's place, the Board named Jim Harlow, who would now wear three hats as Chairman, President and CEO. (When Wayne Parker retired as President on 1973, Harlow assumed the duties as President.)

As Harlow's successor Steve Moore would say later, "Being chairman, CEO, and president is a fine title but it means that if anything goes wrong, it's my fault!"

A Prestigious Award

OG&E's success in dealing with its circumstances in the 1970s and early 1980s won them nationwide recognition as the "Utility of the Year" by *Electric Light & Power* magazine in 1983. OG&E was lauded for its commitment to add

continued on page 110

Cogeneration and Conoco

OG&E had a singular success in developing and building a cogeneration facility with one of OG&E's oldest and largest customers—Conoco. Oklahoma's Continental Oil Company (later shortened to Conoco) was founded in 1875. Pittsburgh, Pennsylvania lawyer-turned-oilman Ernest W. Marland struck oil on Ponca Indian lands. Marland obtained drilling rights on the Indian land and after he brought in the gusher, established the Marland Oil Company, merged with Continental in 1929, and built a refinery at Ponca City. Oklahoma's success in oil and natural gas became legend, fueling the state's increasingly rapid development.

The Conoco refinery had become OG&E's second-largest customer. By the 1990s, Conoco found it had excess fuel capacity at its facility in an era of dropping oil prices. Often, methane gas was simply burned off into the atmosphere as part of the refining process. Perhaps that methane could be used for something productive.

The company worked closely with OG&E to develop a first-of-its-kind power plant, located on Conoco property. The new power plant used the waste methane as fuel to drive the electric generators. The generation equipment was controlled and supervised by OG&E engineering staff locally and remotely from the Sooner Station.

In yet another twist, the two 26,000-kilowatt generators produced steam, which was then sold to Conoco for use in the refining processes. OG&E also found the plant produced more power than Conoco needed, so about 40 percent of the power was distributed over the OG&E power grid, available for sale to other customers. OG&E paid Conoco for the amount of methane used to generate the power. The unique and landmark installation was the first time OG&E used "waste refinery gas" to produce electric power, while at the same time selling steam as a power by-product. It also marked the first use of a computerized system to control operating units from another location.

"The Conoco project is a perfect example of the way cogeneration should work," said OG&E's Vice President of Marketing Dick Day after the plant was dedicated.

"This is the way cogeneration makes sense. It's the way it ought to be done."

Cogeneration plant at Conoco in Ponca City.

coal-fueled power production to the traditional natural gas–fueled facilities, combined with the very aggressive and popular conservation and load management programs spearheaded by the Marketing and Consumer Relations Department.

In a congratulatory message to OG&E members describing the award, Harlow said:

Your personal commitment and involvement in the company are absolute musts for our continued success.

We have improved our performance substantially these past few years. You are helping control costs. You are planning better. And we are working together more effectively to make OG&E a healthier company.

An important corner had been turned during a difficult time. The company was no longer losing money, nor as deeply concerned about power supply during peak periods. OG&E had still not completely emerged from the dramatic reversals experienced with the start of the energy crisis in 1973. Through very hard work and by implementing

OG&E's 1983 recognition as Utility of the Year is shown in an issue of the *Electric Light & Power* newsletter displayed by Jim Harlow.

The Muskogee Business Office.

very tough decisions, the corner had been turned.

Still, OG&E would face additional hurdles during the next few years. The company needed to change even more in order to build on its successes.

More Coal, More Expansion

The immediate improvement in company fortunes allowed OG&E to once again resume expansion plans. The construction budget had been curtailed during the financial crisis.

Construction on the Muskogee coal-fired Unit No. 6, originally authorized in March 1978, was dramatically scaled back in November 1979. But with the reversal of fortunes in the early 1980s, construction resumed and the new unit began operations June 18, 1984. A boon to the local Muskogee economy resulted as OG&E increased staffing by 100 people, bringing the total members employed at Muskogee to 380. The Muskogee Unit No. 6 was brought online ahead of the revised schedule and under budget. The newly completed coal-fired plant enabled OG&E to provide a more cost-efficient source of power.

OG&E faced serious questions when it asked the regulatory commission for several rate increases to help pay for the plant. Although several increases had been granted by the Oklahoma Corporation

continued on page 113

Of Prairie Dogs and Geese

Animal rights and protection of endangered species may have not readily entered the minds of OG&E's early leaders. They were most concerned about keeping the tender company afloat in a reckless era of stock manipulation and whimsical government interference. But the concept of dual land use came into the public utility vernacular around mid-twentieth century. OG&E was part of the process:

In the 1960s, the 1,350-acre cooling reservoir for the Seminole plant was named Lake Konawa and opened to the public for recreational boating and fishing.

In 1982, OG&E imported a flock of 246 Canada geese to colonize the sprawling Sooner Power Station near Ponca City. In the 1970s, Canada geese were an endangered species in the United States. A large flock was found living near a power plant in the northern United States at a time when many thought they were headed for extinction—or already extinct. The geese were trucked to Ponca City and allowed to graze on the available foraging land surrounding the plant.

In the early 1980s, a prairie dog town was dis-covered on the Mustang plant property west of Oklahoma City. Although not an endangered species, the prairie dogs at Mustang were part of a man-and-animal saga that has proved emotional and furious over the years—particularly for residents and ranch owners. At Mustang, the prairie dogs built a typical "village" of underground passageways for their living quarters and for safety from predators, such as coyotes, bobcats, predatory birds, and foxes.

Commission, the late 1970s and early 1980s were a time of extreme inflation, constantly cutting into OG&E's ability to collect payment rates equal to the always-increasing expenses involved in producing power.

This was a complex problem, intricate to explain to a public weary from a series of rate increases. Worse, the complex story was difficult to spread through traditional media sources.

Enogex—Putting the "Gas" Back in Oklahoma Gas and Electric

In fall 1986, OG&E's leadership team boldly enhanced the company's ability to generate profits apart from regulated power production. Looking back to the firm's roots as a supplier of both electric power and natural gas, OG&E purchased the Mustang Fuel Corporation in September 1986.

Mustang Fuel was originally formed to bring natural gas to OG&E's Mustang, Oklahoma power complex. By the mid-1980s Mustang Fuel supplied natural gas through a three-thousand-mile pipeline network, much of it to OG&E's seven natural gas–fired power plants. This new, unregulated venture became a wholly owned subsidiary of OG&E.

Shortly after acquiring Mustang Fuel, OG&E renamed the unit Enogex Inc. With the purchase, two operating subsidiaries of Enogex were formed.

Enogex Products Corporation manufactured and marketed byproducts of the natural gas refinement process. Whereas "natural gas" is methane, other items can be removed prior to delivery, such as propane, butane, ethane, isobutene, and "natural gasoline." Enogex Products Corporation marketed these byproducts to other industries for use in rubber production, plastics, paints, fertilizers, and as fuel for outdoor grills, farm equipment, and home heating devices, thus providing yet another potential—and unregulated—revenue stream.

The Enogex Services Corporation oversaw the pipeline delivery process.

Although OG&E's move back into natural gas did not involve sales to residential consumers, as it had in the company's infancy, it was nonetheless a return to a portion of the company's expertise for the first time since the company sold off all its natural gas assets in 1928.

The Need to Reorganize

OG&E was in a vise, pinched by rising construction, financing, and production costs and the inability to charge power rates sufficient to meet the expenses. An economic downturn compounded the problem—especially severe as Oklahoma oil prices plummeted creating a

Kenny King, environmental analyst, Enogex.

catastrophe for the state's premier business. Something had to change.

In a message to OG&E members, Harlow said:

We can never go back to the old ways of doing business at OG&E.

The downturn has resulted in our first net customer loss since the Great Depression. Coinciding with this lack of growth, we have experienced declining sales of electricity and increasing competition from other electric suppliers.

Because of this . . . we had to reduce the price of our product and cut our construction program. . . . We are forced into cutting costs in order to compete.

One obvious answer is to reduce the number of employees.

With that, OG&E members faced a bitter pill. To be competitive, OG&E had to downsize.

Downsizing

A special team of OG&E members conducted a complete top-down study of all jobs within the company. Their assignment was to determine the minimum number and classification of jobs absolutely necessary to permit the organization to continue its core business. The committee recommended an overall cut of at least 620 of the 4,600 jobs throughout the organization.

On April 14, 1987, an early retirement option was offered to veteran OG&E members. The move, dubbed the Special Retirement Opportunity Program, offered enhanced benefits incentives. Four hundred and sixty-five took advantage of it by May 1988. An additional 119 employees departed through an established Voluntary Separation Program.

The reduction in work force was a deeply troubling experience for many OG&E members and their families. Helping explain the circumstances to members, Harlow said, "We are in a period when we no longer need the kind of work force we used to have. The company's overall human resource needs have changed radically.

"Streamlining the organization puts the customer with people who are most directly involved with their needs.

"So, reduced rates, streamlined organization, and new ways we are doing things are making us more competitive."

Besides the reduction in work force, OG&E's management also consolidated what had been six geographic administrative regions down to three, thus removing several layers of supervisory personnel while maintaining the same response time to emergencies and attentiveness to customer needs.

The End Results of Hard Decisions

By the end of 1988, OG&E had reduced its total work force by one thousand down to thirty-six hundred. It was an unprecedented and dramatic change in the way the company did business. The traditional four-person work crews had been reduced, wherever possible, to two-person crews.

The devotion to customer service was enhanced as the company opened a twenty-four-hours-a-day, seven-days-a-week customer service call center.

The relentless search for new energy resulted in the formation of the Enogex Exploration Company in November 1988. The unit continued the search for natural gas opportunities.

Only a determined work ethic could have withstood the pressures brought on during 1973 through the 1980s. For the company's first seventy years, with notable exceptions, there had been constant expansion, opportunity and growth. But as soon as Harlow took over as OG&E president in

1973, he guided the company's change in order to keep its commitment to the customers and shareowners, alike. Harlow was equal to the task of coordinating the most uncertain times in anyone's memory.

By the beginning of the 1990s, OG&E had turned things around. OG&E was a team that had—and would—prevail. But the 1990s would not be without challenges. They would test the company yet again. ■

Scott Boyd, meter reader, Marketing and Customer Care, enters data into a "roadrunner" device.

OG&E has been an industry pioneer in many areas of policy and operation.

In the late 1960s, OG&E began the policy of underground installation of electric lines for residential customers free of charge under ordinary circumstances.

A few years earlier, OG&E became one of the first utilities in the nation to promote electric water heating and electric space heating. These promotional programs resulted in rate discounts for the customers and proved very popular.

OGE Sports

Throughout OG&E's history, members and retirees have been encouraged to participate in company-sponsored activities. One example is the company's sponsorship of sports teams. OG&E has at one time or another sponsored and encouraged golf, bowling, basketball, softball, baseball, and tennis.

OG&E golf tournaments date as far back as 1931, growing out of interdepartmental golf events. Subsequent tournaments have been held in almost every year so that the 2001 OG&E golf tournament was actually the sixty-seventh in the company's long history.

Although baseball teams and tennis tournaments are first mentioned in the late 1920s and early 1930s, evidence suggests that organized company-sponsored events took place years before, especially baseball. A 1931 issue of the *Oklahoma Meter* mentions that sixteen members played in the men's singles tennis tournament held August 17 to 22 of that year, while the Stores Garage Line baseball team won the league championship with an undefeated record.

In September 1935, none other than OG&E President George A. Davis rolled the first ball in the inaugural OG&E bowling season. Held at Oklahoma City's Brantley's Bowling Alley, the event was heralded as a turning point in the Depression. Bowling has continued as a popular activity for OG&E members ever since.

Top: OG&E baseball players in 1928.

OG&E Oklahoma City "B" (Bowling) League, 1939–1940.

Right: OG&E Women's Basketball Team and coaches, 1928–1929.

Softball events have been less structurally organized; however, detailed records of events have been kept since 1979.

Basketball is a relative latecomer to the OG&E spectrum of organized sports; the first OG&E basketball tournament was held in February 1983. Since then, basketball has attracted a growing number of OG&E members as trophies are awarded each year for the championship team.

OG&E members participate in the Corporate Challenge, a nationwide competition designed to encourage fitness, health, and teamwork among corporations and businesses in communities. In 1990, OG&E members took the top trophy in their division, competing in nineteen events including running, volleyball, basketball, and tug-of-war.

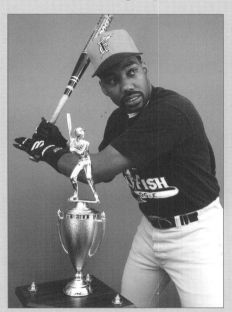

Other less formal events have been regularly held, including impromptu pick-up games at company picnics and walking events for charity organizations, such as the "Walk for Heart."

Tena Slaughter, clerk, Market Solutions, coordinates many of the company's sporting events including the Corporate Challenge.

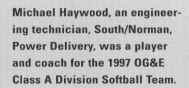

Michael Haywood, an engineering technician, South/Norman, Power Delivery, was a player and coach for the 1997 OG&E Class A Division Softball Team.

Left: Retiree George McFarlane, former manager, Economic Development, often participated in the company's bowling tournaments.

Right: Hank Johnson enjoys a swing at a company-sponsored golf tournament.

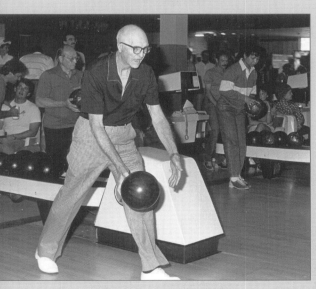

OG&E's Part in the 1989 Summer Olympic Festival

OG&E President Jim Harlow continually stressed community and volunteer involvement throughout his life. Practicing what he preached, Harlow's list of volunteer endeavors impresses even the most hardened.

But his volunteerism became an OG&E company-wide event in the summer of 1989 as Oklahoma played host to the Olympic Festival. Held each summer for three consecutive summers in the years leading up to the quadrennial summer Olympic Games, the Olympic Festival features ten days of competition in thirty-seven sporting events.

A highlight is the community torch run. On June 17, 1989, the Olympic Torch was ignited atop Pike's Peak and eventually made its way through 260 Oklahoma towns in seventy-seven counties of the Sooner State.

Beginning July 21, more than 400 OG&E employees will be wearing something a little different. It may not be as different as this photo, but you get the idea. They're going to be volunteers for the U.S. Olympic Festival in and around Oklahoma City.

OG&E is helping to sponsor the Festival and we're proud that hundreds of OG&Eers have volunteered their own time to be a part of this great event. OK89 will focus national and world-wide attention on our area and we hope you'll attend as many events as possible. We know you'll have a great time at the nation's premier sports spectacular of 1989.

July 21st-30th, 1989
Oklahoma City, OK

Dozens of OG&E members were among the more than fifteen thousand volunteers participating in the festival. Many served as torch carriers, running the Olympic Flame around OG&E properties such as the Sooner and Muskogee plants. Other OG&E members served as photographers, parking lot attendants, scorekeepers, and computer operators, among many other tasks. They did it all on their free time and loved the experience.

"It was a once-in-a-lifetime experience," said OG&E member Bill Busch. "The Olympic spirit was contagious."

Left: OG&E's participation in the U.S. Olympic Festival held in Oklahoma City in 1989 featured this advertisement.

Above: Terry Scroggins, reliability technician, Power Supply Services, was one of twenty-six torch runners at the Muskogee plant as part of the 1989 Olympic Festival in Oklahoma.

OG&E *Currents*

Currents is published monthly for the customers of OG&E Electric Services ● March 2001

"Whose Power Is Restored First During Major Storms?"

Hospitals, Police and Fire Departments and the Media

Sometimes severe storms cause large numbers of customers to lose their electricity. At OG&E, we follow a very specific plan to restore electric service to customers. Our first concern is safety.

Here are our priorities:
1. Hospitals and other health care providers, police and fire departments and the media.
2. Failure at a key point in our system that affects thousands of customers, such as transmission or distribution lines – our "main highways" of power.
3. Individual lines.

Weather conditions, accessibility to damaged areas, the time of day and environmental issues are among the many factors that determine the amount of time it takes to restore power. These factors can affect each outage, which greatly complicates our ability to predict restoration times.

Here's A Look At Our Order Of Restoration

To get the power back on during a storm, OG&E works from the source of the power outward.

The diagram below shows the typical order of power restoration on OG&E's system. In this case, restoration would begin from the transmission line and progress from there.

We would begin at point A on the transmission line. With the line out, none of the houses can have power restored. Next, we would fix the problem at B on the main distribution line running out of the substation. Houses 2, 3, 4 and 5 are affected by this problem. Once the problem at B has been fixed, we would go to the tap line at C, that affects houses 4 and 5. Finally, we would repair the service line at D to house 1.

POWER RESTORATION SEQUENCE

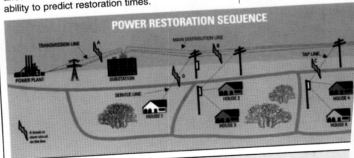

"Customer Service, How May We Help You..."

Actually, generating and distributing electricity is only a part of what OG&E is all about.

Providing the best possible service to our

FEBRUARY 1996

"Need Money To Buy A Heat Pump Or Water Heater?"

OG&E electric services

OG&E *Currents* is a monthly publication with consumer information for the customers of OG&E Electric Services.

"Every contact with every customer must be a quality experience. We want our customers to be satisfied with us because we treat them better and have more to offer than our competitors. . . ."

OG&E *Meter*,
December 1990

CHAPTER 9

We've Got the Power: 1989–1996

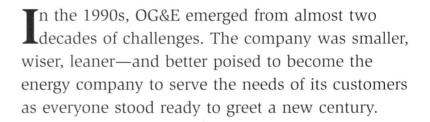

In the 1990s, OG&E emerged from almost two decades of challenges. The company was smaller, wiser, leaner—and better poised to become the energy company to serve the needs of its customers as everyone stood ready to greet a new century.

As 1990 dawned, OG&E's CEO Jim Harlow announced an idea program designed to create a cascade of imaginative ideas from members. Dubbed "We've Got the Power," the effort sought ways to increase revenues and cut expenses.

Teams of OG&E members devised efficiency ideas, which qualified them for a series of attractive incentive prizes. Should their ideas save the company at least $1,000 within the first year, they'd win points for merchandise awards. OG&E members enthusiastically participated, generating 450 solid ideas worth $10 million in annual increased revenue or cost-savings to the company.

As an extra benefit, the brainstorming sessions produced almost 3,300 ideas related to safety, customer service, and quality improvement.

Jim Harlow at the Customer Service Call Center with Customer Service Consultant Joslyn Burkhalter.

Economic Development Plans

Following the successful "We've Got the Power" idea campaign, the company entered a period of outreach to the community and to customers. To help shake off the effects of an economic recession in 1990, OG&E structured several recovery plans to assist its large customers, which helped increase sales.

First, the Certified Industrial Parks program offered direct assistance to any of the 260 Oklahoma and Arkansas communities to plan or standardize their industrial parks. The OG&E program certified communities based on factors desirable to businesses. An OG&E Certified Industrial Park was a benchmark throughout the Oklahoma and Arkansas service area.

Phyllis Durbin, supervisor of Mailing Services, checks the final product of a new billing and mailing system in 1991.

Second, OG&E offered a Matching Grant Program. Those communities or companies who sought to purchase or upgrade land, buildings, or equipment to enhance their plant or industrial park could apply to OG&E for grants up to $30,000. These OG&E grants also served as a platform to attract state and federal economic development funding.

Kinzie Industries, an Alva, Oklahoma airplane and helicopter parts manufacturer, was the first business recipient of a Matching Grant.

A third means to assist industrial and commercial clients was the ReSource Program, devised near the end of 1990. A specialized team of OG&E members was available to advise participants in many areas of business consulting and energy management. The ReSource Program was built with the underlying belief that as businesses and communities profit and prosper, OG&E's electric load should increase with greater economic health in the region.

Continued Progress

In 1991, OG&E introduced yet another cost-savings effort as the monthly billings to OG&E customers were electronically bar-coded as they were processed. The bar-coding arrangements with the U.S. Postal Service saved more than $100,000 annually in postage costs in billing OG&E's 650,000 customers.

Still another innovative means to reduce load was Demand-Side Management (DSM), a program introduced for OG&E customers in late 1991 and early 1992. DSM empowers customers to regulate their own energy use—especially those who require less power at peak periods. Participants allowed OG&E to make more power available on the total power grid without generating more power or building new power plants.

In conjunction with this energy use cooperation, OG&E installed a leading edge monitoring system in 1992. Called THOR (Trouble History and Outage Resolution), the system specifically pinpointed exact locations of any failed equipment. THOR also was a boon in times of emergency. Over the years, OG&E averaged seven major storms a year resulting in power outages. THOR achieved much more efficient assignment of repair crews, quicker restoration of electric service where it had been interrupted, and significant cost-savings to the company.

Quality Process

OG&E's successful experiment in small work team approaches to problem solving, as seen in the 1990 "We've Got the Power" program, was revisited and expanded in mid-1992 as the Quality Process (introduced by W. Edwards Demming). The company once again analyzed how it conducted its business in light of the quality and nature of customer service. More consolidation followed:

First, the Corporate Communications Department reorganized later that year. The restructuring brought together employee communications, media relations, research, and advertising under a single department.

Next, the Environmental Affairs Department was revamped to find better ways to communicate information with and to internal customers—members working in power plants and regions. The purpose was to help educate and explain constantly changing environmental laws and regulations and enlist the participation of local-area members in addressing and observing the myriad regulations.

Later, the Quality Process expanded to regional areas of the company—often on the individual plant level.

A real-life case of the effectiveness of the Quality Process took place in 1993 when Wal-Mart decided to build one of its megastore SuperCenters in

Pat Fuller, senior engineer (left), and Morris Lovett, design engineer, were among the members who received Quality Process training.

Top: Tammy Turnipseed, design engineer, and M. H. Hakim, senior engineer, put their Quality Process training to use.

continued on page 126

Reddy Kilowatt, OG&E's Mascot for a Half-Century

For half the history of the company, OG&E made use of a friendly symbol, a stick person of lightning bolts and a light bulb head—Reddy Kilowatt. Reddy made his first appearance at OG&E in September 1936 as a tangible and whimsical personification of electrical service—a product impossible to see or hold.

Reddy Kilowatt was not exclusive to OG&E; rather, he was the symbol of many investor-owned electric utilities. He started life in 1926, ten years before he was introduced to OG&E. The creation of Ashton B. Collins, merchandising manager for the Alabama Power Company, Reddy Kilowatt was an attempt to humanize the idea of electric service. Reddy Kilowatt went on to grace billings, advertising, billboards, premiums, clothing, communications, employee newsletters, and the OG&E logo. At one time, OG&E staffers would take turns playing the part of Reddy Kilowatt at various functions with a yellow full-body costume. A huge flashing electric representation of Reddy Kilowatt graced the side of the OG&E building in bright lights for decades.

During his heyday, Reddy Kilowatt was the mascot and symbol of more than two hundred U.S. investor-owned electric utilities, as well as those in several foreign countries. The symbol was so successful that Reddy's creator, Ashton Collins, incorporated it into Reddy Kilowatt, Inc., and licensed the mascot's use to utilities.

In the 1990s, times and symbols had changed so that OG&E no longer used Reddy Kilowatt as a corporate mascot. However, Reddy still lives, used by other utilities, and continues to be licensed as a trademark of RKC, a wholly owned subsidiary of Xcel Energy Corporation.

In the 1930s, Reddy's likeness became part of the OG&E building sign.

Save energy and money with ECHO and AWARD.

An **ECHO** energy audit shows you what your home needs . . . and OG&E's **AWARD**, which stands for: Audit and Weatherization Aid Reduce Demand, helps you pay for it.

Call your nearest OG&E office and request an ECHO audit. The audit costs $15. You will receive a computerized analysis of how your home uses and loses energy. You will also be given an estimate of how much energy you will save when you make improvements.

You'll start saving NOW with this free energy kit.

An energy kit is included with the ECHO audit of your home and includes materials you can put to work immediately: Caulking gun and caulking compound, weatherstripping, electric outlet sealers.

OG&E's AWARD program will pay you $200 for every kilowatt saved.

Audit and Weatherization Aid Reduce Demand

When any or all of such qualifying improvements as insulation, storm doors or windows and more energy-efficient central air conditioning are installed, OG&E will pay you $200 per kilowatt saved. Chances are you'll also qualify for income tax credits, too. And remember . . . . this is the season air conditioners begin to fail and maybe you've been thinking of getting a new one. Have an ECHO audit first, then get OG&E's help to buy a more efficient unit.

Call your nearest OG&E office for an ECHO home energy audit.

We'll make an appointment for your ECHO home energy audit and you'll be on your way to saving energy and money with ECHO and AWARD.

Reddy Kilowatt® became part of the OG&E logo in the 1980s.

OG&E and Electric Vehicles

In the mid-1990s, OG&E worked with the University of Oklahoma and Electrosource, a company that makes lead acid batteries to promote awareness of electric vehicles.

Three electric vehicles joined the OG&E fleet: A GMC G-Van, a Chrysler mini-van, and a Ford Escort. All three battery-powered vehicles became a showcase of the OG&E-sponsored Oklahoma Electric Vehicle Institute for Research and Development.

OG&E later sponsored research with Oklahoma University to produce a two-hundred-mile-per-hour electric race car.

Ada, Oklahoma. The area is also served by a local electric co-op. Local members, fresh from the Quality Process experience, immediately formed a team to assess the potential power needs of the complex, the construction costs involved in delivering the power supply, and a timetable to supply the service. By acting quickly on its own initiative, the Ada Quality Process team surveyed the site, produced detailed cost estimates, and approached Wal-Mart with an easement arrangement and service contract. Wal-Mart recognized the potential cost-savings and entered into a five-year service agreement with OG&E.

All this took place before the local power co-op even called on Wal-Mart to solicit its business. In the past, OG&E would have typically waited for the potential consumer to make the first contact. The resulting headquarters-based engineering study would have taken much longer and the delay could have resulted in lost business. By moving the decision-making and initiative process to a local level quality team, OG&E became a more aggressive operator. OG&E members saw first-hand that placing customer service at the top of the "to do" list paid off for not only the client, but for the company as well.

A New Headquarters

By 1992, OG&E headquarters members worked in scattered sites throughout the Oklahoma City area. That year, the company leased 250,000 square feet in the modern Corporate Tower office building at

101 North Robinson Avenue in Oklahoma City. By doing so, all headquarters members were under one roof for the first time in fifteen years. The original building on Harvey, built in the late 1920s and doubled in size in 1958, was insufficient by 1987.

The 1992 move was not the company's last. During the mid-

1990s, OG&E meticulously remodeled and renovated the original building on Harvey Avenue. In 1998, the OG&E team was once again in the original headquarters—this time retrofitted with state-of-the-art systems and offices. The office work environment now sported ergonomic work-stations instead of the traditional desks and credenzas. A gala open house christened the return to the company's legendary building. The exterior and common area Art Deco appointments were restored and refreshed. The work areas were "cutting edge."

Other Developments

By this time, Enogex had passed the five-year mark, and the company celebrated the good news. The natural gas production, pipeline,

OG&E Oklahoma City Headquarters relocated to Corporate Tower in the 1990s. Members moved back in 1998 to the original headquarters building at 321 Harvey Avenue after complete renovations.

Left: Work stations at Corporate Headquarters in 1998.

distribution, and service company, wholly owned by OG&E, was a profit center in an unregulated revenue area.

For years, investor-owned utilities had looked toward nonregulated subsidiaries to provide opportunity. There had been some notable and highly embarrassing disasters by other utilities, which had made decisions to acquire insurance companies or savings and loan operations as partners in their house.

OG&E was cautious in forming Enogex from an acquired gas pipeline company. By staying within the power industry and not straying from its roots, OG&E built Enogex into a formidable and reliable partner in overall operations. Expanding operations of this profitable venture, Enogex opened offices in Houston and Chicago in 1990.

Enogex has grown to become the tenth largest natural gas pipeline in the nation.

Corporate Headquarters executive floor.

Twenty Years at the Top

By 1993, Jim Harlow had been the company's leader for twenty years. In that time, he had become a nationally recognized expert and visionary in the power production and investor-owned utility arena. Interviewed by the *Meter* on the eve of this anniversary, Harlow talked about the pressures faced by the company and its response to them. "Our service territory has not grown since the early 1980s due to the downturn in the oil industry and the economy in general. . . . It was not until 1991 that we got back the number of customers we had in 1984."

Integral to OG&E's recovery was the dual thrust of reorganization, resulting in downsizing and the intense use of the Quality Process in customer service. "A team can often generate more ideas, concepts, and successes than an individual could. Team support of an idea tends to make people examine more opportunities to make change," Harlow continued. "Change will help the company continue to succeed."

continued on page 131

Business Resource Center (BRC) members Larry Saxon, specialist, Data Services, and Jan Martin, graphics specialist, view a document for a client. The BRC opened in 1988.

James G. Harlow Jr.: OG&E's Longest-Serving President

The electric utility industry and OG&E were well served to have Jim Harlow as CEO of the company during the most tumultuous decades in the company's history. His steady hand and determined leadership style guided OG&E in uncertain times. The company emerged stronger but leaner in the aftermath.

Harlow was a native Oklahoman, and a graduate of Norman High School and the University of Oklahoma with training in engineering and finance. He was also an honorary graduate of Oklahoma City University. Following two years in the U.S. Navy, Harlow joined OG&E as a research analyst in the Corporate Accounting Department in 1961.

His early work in finance quickly moved into more challenging administrative roles. In 1962, Harlow entered an intense training program that taught him the "customer" side of the business. He read meters, worked in telephone customer service, and even discontinued service to one of his college fraternity brothers.

"I learned that customers are not disembodied voices on the phone, but people who must be worked with," Harlow recalled in a 1995 *Inside* interview. "It is important for all our members to have an awareness of how our customers feel."

Harlow was elected a company officer in 1966, director in 1970, president in 1973, CEO in 1976, and chairman of the Board in 1982. Although the incredible external pressures forced Harlow to devote the vast majority of time to internal company issues, he did still find the time to participate in a myriad of civic, professional, and philanthropic endeavors. The list of honors, boards, and awards is long.

Most impressive was the man. "He kept the company's reputation for integrity spotless and fearless as well as his own," says current OGE CEO Steve Moore about his former boss. "Jim Harlow steered us through all those fundamental changes in the company." And he did it with good people skills, grace, and an incessant curiosity about his work, his industry, and the people who worked for him. His mission was to constantly survey the company for more efficient and effective ways to do business.

For Harlow, the questions he was always asking were: *What is best for company members? What is best for shareowners? What is best for customers?* In a thirty-five-year career with OG&E, he came to personify the company focus on customer service.

As a tribute to Harlow's memory, the University of Oklahoma established the James G. Harlow Jr. Chair in Business Ethics and Community Service in the Price College of Business.

Jim Harlow served OG&E well as president during a tumultuous period in the energy industry.

At the forefront of company changes were the Quality Process teams. They were about to be transformed into an ongoing company initiative called Continuous Improvement. Company operational and cultural change was now to become an OG&E fact of life.

As he spoke on the eve of his twentieth anniversary as president, Harlow could justifiably appreciate the accomplishment brought about on his watch. But for Harlow, an even bigger challenge waited on life's road.

Reorganization and Competition

A second reorganization took place in 1994 resulting in further reductions in force. OG&E would have to grow even leaner to maintain profitability. At the same time, deregulation of the industry loomed large on the energy production and supply horizon. Rates would likely go lower and OG&E would have to cut its costs in a new world of greater competition soon to come.

As a result, a hiring and salary freeze was enacted in April 1994, followed by the second large-scale early retirement offering made to members within seven years of retirement age. By fall 1994, 755 OG&E members accepted early retirement.

In the era of increasing competition, Harlow rallied the troops. "The most difficult challenge is to prepare the Company for competition," he said in a 1994 *Meter* interview. "Through the Quality Process, every person, regardless of his or her job, can improve the Company. The Quality Process is a powerful tool to be used to beat the competition. In order to change our Company, we must all have commitment and get involved."

"Beating the Socks off the Competition" became the goal offered by the Redesign Steering Committee. The challenges:

Providing superior value to our customers and communities.

Earning attractive returns for our shareowners.

Continually challenging ourselves to achieve the highest levels of individual and team performance.

The Day Oklahoma City—and the Nation—Stood Still

No OG&E member working in Oklahoma City will forget what he or she was doing or exactly where they were at 9:02 a.m., Wednesday, April 19, 1995.

OG&E offices were in "temporary" quarters at 101 North Robinson, just a few blocks away from the Alfred P. Murrah Federal Building. All conversations and concentrations halted at that moment as a horrendous explosion shook the area, demolishing the Federal

May 5, 1995

Inside

A biweekly publication for OG&E Electric Services

Time Of Heartache
OG&E Responds To Crisis In Downtown OKC

On a sunny spring morning at 9:02 April 19, a devastating explosion destroyed most of the Alfred P. Murrah Federal Building at Fifth Street and Robinson in downtown Oklahoma City.

In addition to the federal building, more than 220 buildings received damage. Estimates show about 200 people may be found dead and more than 450 were injured as a result of the homemade bomb blast.

Federal authorities are now investigating the tragedy as a domestic terrorist bombing. Sadly, **Danny Blanton**, a fieldman in credit and collections, **Marketing and Customer Services**, lost his wife, **Andrea**, in the explosion.

"Our hearts go out to our members who have lost loved ones during this tragedy," said **Jim Harlow**, chairman of the board and president of OG&E. "Downtown Oklahoma City is where our corporate headquarters is located and is part of what we call home. Few words can describe the great sadness we all feel for our city, state and nation. We can only hope this terrible event brings us closer together as we face the healing that must now go on."

Corporate Tower/Metro

Five blocks south at **Corporate Tower**, 101 N. Robinson, the explosion caused some members to scramble under their desks, while others felt themselves sway with the building. Afterward, most members ran to their windows in time to see fire, black smoke, paper and other debris billowing north on Robinson.

Meanwhile, members from throughout the Oklahoma City area

OG&E responds continued on page 2

The Alfred P. Murrah Federal Building

Building. One hundred sixty-eight innocent and unsuspecting men, women, and children in the building were killed—their lives crushed in the collapse and debris. Terrorism had come to Oklahoma City.

The aftermath of rescue, rebuilding, and caring for victims and their loved ones may have been Oklahoma's finest hours.

OG&E members immediately assembled teams of people to help in many ways. Typical of OG&E's quick and compassionate response to the many weather disasters plaguing their Oklahoma and Arkansas service region, the assistance in this singular disaster may have also been OG&E's greatest endeavor.

OG&E work crews descended upon the site, some without being assigned—they were drawn to it. Live electric wires had to be secured and disconnected, while emergency power had to be restored to help in the rescue effort. One five-person OG&E crew climbed into an underground transformer vault within the demolished and unstable building to disconnect service.

Another OG&E crew used ladders to reach stranded, wounded people on the exposed second floor. Beyond the reach of the truck "basket" the OG&E members guided dazed, bleeding survivors down the ladders to safety, some with clothing torn to shreds because of flying glass shards and debris.

Other OG&E crews strung temporary emergency service lines to provide power to searchlights for the rescue operations. Other crews helped by powering pumps to remove water from the devastated build-

ing's basement.

Seventeen OG&E members were working in a finance and records storage location one block south of the explosion. Windows blew out, light fixtures fell from the ceiling, and debris showered through the work area, luckily hurting no one.

Incredibly, another OG&E member team was lifted by crane to the roof of the still-standing portion of the Federal Building where they attached a portable generator to restart the remaining elevator. Amazingly, the unit did operate, providing firefighters and rescue personnel the ability to access all other parts of the building.

OG&E's highly sophisticated infrared cameras were brought in from Ardmore to help in the search for buried victims, bomb fragments, and structural cracks.

The aftermath of the explosion became a blur as all of Oklahoma City pitched in with single-minded purpose to help in the effort. OG&E's part was one more cog in a truly communitywide team effort. Within weeks, OG&E and its members were to receive commendations and recognition for their work and help in the bombing's horrific aftermath. A special commemorative flag was presented in honor of the OG&E members who worked so selflessly.

OG&E was not untouched by the death and destruction, as Andrea Blanton, wife of OG&E Marketing and Customer

Gary Gardner, supervisor of service restoration, Power Delivery (right), was one of the many OG&E members who worked during the rescue efforts following the bombing of the Alfred P. Murrah Federal Building in 1995.

Effects of the April 19, 1995 bombing are visible on this Harvey Avenue street sign.

Hurricane-force winds of more than ninety-five miles per hour created a carnage of toppled trees and poles during the 1995 wind storm dubbed "Storm of the Century."

Eighty-three circuits in the Oklahoma City area and numerous transmission lines were affected as a result of the storm.

Services fieldman Danny Blanton, lost her life in the explosion.

The following months would once again demonstrate the unflappable Oklahoma optimism as the community moved ahead in healing and rebuilding.

A Summer Shocker

As if OG&E and Oklahoma City had not been through enough, the worst storm in OG&E history swept through during the night hours of July 23, 1995. Winds of almost one hundred miles per hour damaged and destroyed the OG&E power transmission and distribution system. At one time, 175,000 customers were without power.

Fallen tree damage and downed power lines vexed service crews. To restore power and clear the tree limbs, 138 tree-trimming crews were contracted to help in the restoration. OG&E couldn't fix this one alone. To speed the recovery, OG&E called upon neighboring utilities in Oklahoma and adjacent states. More than 1,775 members and contract workers toiled around the clock for nearly a week to restore power and repair damage.

In Oklahoma City, eighty-three circuits and numerous transmission lines were locked out. The Mustang Power Plant sustained severe damage to the roof, cooling tower, and generating unit.

Sadly, OG&E lineman John D. Garrison, a twenty-year veteran of the North District's Power Delivery, lost his life on July 27 after coming in contact with a 7,200-volt electric line.

In dollar cost, the "Storm of the Century" was estimated at $3.5 million.

A Painful Transition

As OG&E ended 1995, Harlow had been through quite a bit since he first took the reins of the company following Wayne Parker's retirement in 1973. As soon as Harlow sat down in the president's chair, the OPEC Oil Embargo began. From that point on, Harlow supervised a company that had experienced financial and regulatory issues, competition from new sources, and wildly fluctuating energy prices.

More industry and company change took place during Harlow's tenure than during any comparable time period in OG&E's ninety-three-year history. It was not surprising that Harlow decided to relinquish the position of president while retaining the roles of CEO and chairman of the Board.

Harlow's successor was Steven E. Moore, then senior vice president of Law and Public Affairs. Moore had been an OG&E member since 1974 following several years as an assistant attorney general for the State of Oklahoma.

"Jim Harlow told me that the company had many engineers and finance people as president in the past, but in his opinion and the board's opinion, the company needed someone with experience in the legislative arena as the industry was moving into a time of deregulation," Moore recalled.

Moore stepped into the role as fifteenth president of OG&E in 1995. He was to have a smooth transition under the tutelage of the man who had held the company's presidency longer than any other. It wasn't to go according to plan.

"We were to have a slow and gradual transition," says Moore about the change in leadership. Because his background was

Work crews gather materials needed to restore power during the 1995 storm.

By 1993, homes had been using OG&E power for ninety-one years.

significantly different from Harlow's, time was given to allow Moore to come "up to speed" on all the aspects of running OG&E.

"And then Jim got sick," Moore explains. "What had been intended as a very patient transition was suddenly accelerated. I went from being the president and chief operating officer to chief executive officer in eight months. Then I became chairman a month after that."

Shortly after cancer was discovered, the sixty-two-year-old Harlow died on June 1, 1996. Harlow had been, up to the time he turned over the company's reins to Moore, the longest-serving CEO of any utility in the nation.

And just as Harlow plunged into a period of change twenty-three years before, Moore stepped into an arena filled with deregulation, cogeneration, and looming energy supply crises. ■

Steve Moore Remembers Jim Harlow

When James Harlow Jr. became the fourteenth president of OG&E in 1973, he stepped into a changing role. For several decades, the president had been a corporate and community goodwill ambassador, giving speeches, making and accepting civic awards, and serving as a public presence. OG&E would hum along, expanding power production, building new plants, and always lowering rates.

But for Harlow, that quickly changed upon his selection as president, with the effects of the 1973 oil crisis. The events began price, supply, environmental, and regulatory changes that buffeted the electric power industry.

Steve Moore, OG&E's fifteenth president and Harlow's successor, worked closely with Harlow and recalls his challenges and how he measured up to them.

"Things started changing in the mid-1970s, right when Harlow was elected president," Moore explained from a vantage point twenty-five years later. "That was when the federal government started forming an energy policy and required utilities to build certain kinds of power plants. That was compounded by the OPEC [Organization of Petroleum Exporting Countries] cartel's volatility on oil supplies and prices. Even worse, this happened at a time when we had decided to build a new, expensive coal-fired plant and were requesting increased rates.

"Harlow saw the industry at its best and at its most difficult. Through it all, he kept the company on a firm course and maintained OG&E's integrity— as well as his own—as spotless and fearless!" And through the years of unprecedented challenge,

Harlow steered the company through a significant change.

"The secret to his success was his excellent judgment coupled with a willingness, even an eagerness, to change with the times," Moore continues. Harlow dealt with widespread change in the industry, pressures from market forces and regulation, and eventually the significant downsizing of the company.

Focus, intensity, innovation. Good words to describe Jim Harlow. Good words to describe OG&E.

Jim Harlow, seated, and Steve Moore.

"It will take the right kind of tools, skills and confidence to get to the top in a deregulated environment. But heights don't scare us. We've scaled a lot of them in 95 years."

OGE Energy Corp.
1996 Annual Report

CHAPTER 10

Coping with a New World: 1996–2001

In the 1990s, states all across the country and even the U.S. Congress began moving toward deregulation of the electric utility industry. OG&E was initially opposed to such a move, but after careful study, the company went on the record publicly in 1996 supporting electric deregulation—if done correctly.

Steve Moore outlined guiding principles designed to accomplish that aim in his letter to shareowners that year. "We believe that deregulation must provide true customer choice through universal open access. For that to happen, five critical issues must be addressed.

- Deregulation must occur at the same time as in surrounding states and under the same terms.
- Stranded costs must be recovered.
- A level playing field must be established for all competitors so that they can operate under the same rules.
- The role of regulators must be restructured to manage the newly created competitive environment.
- There must be no exceptions to the new rules.

"It's only after these issues are resolved that our customers and shareowners will be able to enjoy the full benefits that are possible under deregulation."

OG&E became actively involved in the deregulation debate in Oklahoma, Arkansas, and at the federal level as laws were passed calling for full customer choice of electric providers in 2002 in the states OG&E served.

By 2001, however, the wave of deregulation began to stall as California, one of the first states to deregulate, began experiencing severe problems. Those closest to the issue recognized that California's problems had little to do with

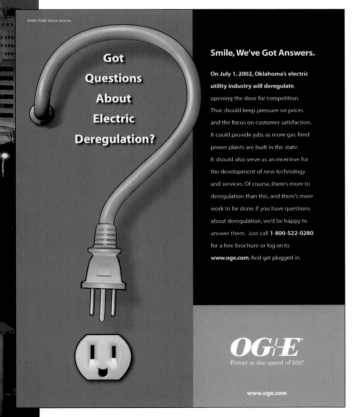

Left: Downtown Oklahoma City is the corporate headquarters of OGE Energy Corp. Inset: OGE advertisement used to promote deregulation.

continued on page 141

©2000 OG&E Electric Services

Got Questions About Electric Deregulation?

Smile, We've Got Answers.

On July 1, 2002, Oklahoma's electric utility industry will deregulate, opening the door for competition. That should keep pressure on prices and the focus on customer satisfaction. It could provide jobs as more gas-fired power plants are built in the state. It should also serve as an incentive for the development of new technology and services. Of course, there's more to deregulation than this, and there's more work to be done. If you have questions about deregulation, we'd be happy to answer them. Just call **1-800-522-0280** for a free brochure or log on to **www.oge.com**. And get plugged in.

OG&E
Power at the speed of life.™

www.oge.com

Top: Jim Wilson, director of Governmental Affairs, at the nation's Capitol in Washington, D.C.

Right: Members participate in Root Learning, which used an Olympics simulation motif to give an overview of the electric utility industry and the concept of deregulation.

deregulation and were more directly related to longstanding supply shortages and an improperly designed electricity market. Nevertheless, national publicity about California's problems placed deregulation on hold throughout most of the country including Oklahoma and Arkansas. As 2001 came to an end, both states were conducting reviews of deregulation and only Texas continued toward full customer choice in 2002.

By 1999, many OG&E service vehicles were equipped with computers. Pictured is Montie Ratliff, service representative, Power Delivery.

A New Era—And a Big Deal

In 1996, OG&E was ready for the next steps. A rate reduction request was filed with the Oklahoma Corporation Commission. The commission unanimously approved the proposal in an unusually brief six months. With the stage set, OG&E strategically reorganized itself in 1996. The ninety-five-year-old Oklahoma Gas and Electric Company became part of a new holding company, OGE Energy Corp.

The company's leadership team decided to establish "business units" to best serve customers and shareowners. This business unit strategy had three entities under the OGE Energy Corp. umbrella:

OG&E Electric Services included electric power delivery, supply, and marketing.

OGE Energy Resources members market energy-related products and services. Shown is Kathryn Henline, Energy Analyst II.

Enogex operated the network of natural gas distribution pipelines as well as production, gathering, processing, and marketing.

Origen Inc. was created to market energy-related products and services.

Although further changes and refinements in this new operating structure took place during the next few years, OGE Energy Corp. had clearly and decisively painted a portrait of twenty-first-century operations. The company had the confidence to succeed in any future energy business environment, whether deregulated or otherwise.

SAP and the World Wide Web

To further assist in the transitional environment, the company incorporated new computer applications. In 1996, an enterprise software application was

continued on page 143

OGE Energy Corp. Today

OGE Energy Corp. in 2002 is a collection of companies. With roots dating back to before Oklahoma statehood, the company was restructured in 1996 to better serve customers in Oklahoma and western Arkansas.

OGE Energy Corp. is a holding company parent to OG&E Electric Services and Enogex, Inc. Steve Moore is Chairman, President, and CEO.

OG&E Electric Services is the trade name for Oklahoma Gas and Electric Company and is a regulated electric utility company with more than seven hundred thousand retail customers in Oklahoma and western Arkansas. It has additional wholesale customers throughout the region.

OG&E's electricity comes from eight company-owned power plants plus purchased power, and is delivered across an interconnected transmission and distribution system that spans thirty thousand square miles serving 274 cities and towns.

Al M. Strecker is executive vice president and chief operating officer for OGE Energy Corp. and OG&E Electric Services. James R. Hatfield is senior vice president and chief financial officer for OGE Energy Corp. and OG&E Electric Services.

Enogex is a nonregulated natural gas production, gathering, transportation, processing, and marketing business. Enogex does not provide retail gas sales.

With the 1999 acquisition of Transok LLC, Enogex now has more than ten thousand miles of intrastate pipeline, combined with interests in eight processing plants. Enogex ranks as the tenth-largest natural gas transportation company in North America. Roger A. Farrell is president and chief executive officer of Enogex Inc.

OGE Energy Resources Inc. was created on April 1, 1997, to market energy-related products and services. OGE Energy Resources specializes in analysis, trading, and risk management. Operating in the national commodities markets for electricity and natural gas, Energy Resources plays a key role in optimizing the generation, transmission, and pipeline assets of OGE Energy. David E. Garcia is group president of OGE Energy Resources Inc.

acquired from SAP (Systems, Applications, and Products in Data Processing). This new software streamlined work processes in Customer Care and Power Delivery. OGE became the first utility in the nation to integrate three separate systems:

- Customer Care System (CCS).
- Computer-Aided Dispatching and Scheduling/Outage Management System (CADS/OMS).

- Geographic Enterprise Management System (GEMS).

The integration involved scores of members, but once onboard and up to speed, SAP was another step in the direction of reducing costs, incorporating more flexible billing, and providing real-time customer information.

Through SAP, OGE Energy's increased efficiency placed it far above competition. It was a tangible display of "Beating the Socks off the Competition."

OGE Energy entered cyberspace in the spring of 1996. The Internet portal www.oge.com was started to further increase customer communication, offering another avenue to provide service, answer questions, and promote the good name and the OGE Energy brand.

By mid-year 1996, OGE Energy unveiled MemberNet, an inhouse intranet communications tool for OGE Energy members companywide. Eventually, all corporate and business unit information could be found on the MemberNet as well as print archives.

Concerns About Enid

In 1997, OG&E Electric Services faced an unexpected situation, partially fueled by the continuing awareness of deregulation. OG&E's twenty-five-year franchise to provide electric service to the Enid community was set to expire. Voters typically renew

OG&E's franchises every twenty-five years. OG&E had provided power to Enid for more than eighty years. This time, the City of Enid expressed interest in buying the local electric system from OG&E instead of renewing the franchise.

A small, vocal group had convinced several of the Enid city leaders to proceed with a buyout. They were convinced a city-owned electric system could generate revenue for the community. However, more than ten thousand local residents signed on to a committee opposing the purchase, calling instead for continued reliable service from OG&E.

In one of the largest voter turnouts in Enid history, the populace voted for a new twenty-five-year franchise for OG&E.

A New Challenge at Century's End

By the final year of the twentieth century, OGE had confronted severe pressures, dealt with them, and emerged stronger and more respected than before.

Not that the challenges were over.

On May 3, 1999, a series of violent storms, including an F5-category tornado, spinning horrific winds of more than three hundred miles per hour, flattened many areas, including OGE's Sooner Station transmission lines. Fifty-seven massive transmission line towers were bent and twisted as the brutal storm ravaged the power distribution system, which supplied a significant portion of Oklahoma City's electricity.

The overnight onslaught spawned fifty-one tornadoes, which traveled for thirty-eight miles. In the aftermath, forty-four people were killed, hundreds were injured, and twenty-two hundred homes were totally destroyed.

One OGE member, David Henry, a seventeen-year veteran of the company, lost his life while protecting his wife and dog as the massive storm struck their home in Moore, Oklahoma.

OGE facilities suffered $16 million in damages. In an enormous corporate effort of tireless members, OGE restored all the lines by June 10. More than 900 OGE members were assisted by 250 reinforcements from other utility companies.

Incredibly, less than a month after the massive May 3 storms, a tornado directly hit the Muskogee Power Plant, demolishing part of the installation and taking the plant offline. With the peak summer demand

time only a few weeks away, OGE crews worked around the clock restoring power and rebuilding parts within the plant. The only injury was a sprained ankle. The heroes again were the OGE members who quickly restored service despite repeated onslaughts of an unforgiving Mother Nature.

OGE's response to the 1999 weather calamities earned the company's members a top national award. The Edison Electric Institute presented their Emergency Response Award to OGE in 2000, citing the company as "a model for electric utilities everywhere." The company was awarded the Emergency Response Award again in 2001 for its restoration efforts during the Christmas 2000 ice storm and the Memorial Day 2001 windstorm.

Another Acquisition

In July 1999, Enogex completed the purchase of Transok LLC. The $701 million acquisition brought what had been Oklahoma's second-largest pipeline (Enogex had been the state's third largest) into OGE Energy.

Transok started life in 1955 as a natural gas supplier to Public Service Company of Oklahoma (PSO), a Central and South West Corporation (CSW), which turned around and purchased Transok in 1961. CSW sold Transok in 1996 to Tejas Energy, a subsidiary of Royal Dutch/Shell Group, which divested its holdings three years later.

The timing was grand for OGE. The ambitious purchase (at what was described as "a stupendous bargain") catapulted Enogex into the top ten pipeline companies in the nation, with more than 10,000 miles of pipeline. When purchased, Transok alone produced 35,000 barrels a day of natural gas liquids. Together, Enogex with Transok had impressive combined assets:

- 6,500 miles of gathering pipeline
- 3,500 miles of transmission pipeline
- 3 billion cubic feet per day transmission capability
- Fifteen gas processing plants
- 1.2 billion cubic-feet of natural gas processing capability
- 23 billion cubic-feet of gas storage capability. ■

Y2K— The Nonevent of the Century

The year 1999 ended with a party of sorts. But not necessarily a New Year's Eve party. It was a Y2K party, as OGE Energy members geared up for the biggest nonevent in centuries. Worldwide fears of Y2K computer glitches threatened to throw the power-generating industry and other businesses and industries into powerlessness. The predictions of doom proved unfounded.

Taking the concerns literally, OGE Energy members did an exhaustive job checking, testing, preparing, and developing backup systems should the worst happen as the calendar flipped from December 31, 1999, to January 1, 2000. Among the concerns were fears that computers and programs would not recognize the digits "2000," or somehow mistake the year for 1900, thus resetting parameters or worse, deleting information, programs, or procedures.

OGE Energy took the Y2K challenge very seriously, considering the possible consequences. A Y2K Readiness Team from all business units met regularly to chart the anticipated needs for the century (and millennium) changeover.

To prepare, the company invested more than $30 million in planning and preparing. The moves taken included replacing the mainframe computer, meticulously identifying all systems which could be affected, making corrections as necessary, and incorporating new computer software governing everything from billing to tracking inventories. A highly visible public relations campaign assured OG&E customers of all the readiness measures.

Heightened anticipation, fueled by live television reports from the OGE Energy headquarters, greeted the extra members who worked overnight on New Year's Eve. When the 1900s sailed off into history at the final strike of twelve, OGE members were confident their hard work and preparation had paid off.

Just as many others experienced across the land, nothing happened. Absolutely nothing. OG&E had succeeded and the Y2K party was for naught. But the willingness of OG&E members to give up the historic evening with their families and friends was a tribute to their "can-do" spirit of cooperation.

Several Corporate Communications members spent New Year's Eve 1999 answering customers' Y2K-related telephone calls.

Retiring to the Active Life

OGE Energy's members maintain their camaraderie and involvement even after they complete their professional careers. Retirees often begin new careers and continue to meet with old friends and co-workers. They also get involved in their communities.

Mackey Lantz is currently president of one of the Oklahoma City OGE Retirees' Breakfast Clubs. He directs the activities of the eighty to one hundred OG&E retirees who meet on the third Tuesday of each month. Breakfast Club programs offer advice on financial or health topics. Occasional group tours entertain the group, who also join together in charitable donations and work.

Jack Rector retired from OGE Energy in 1987, but continues an active life as a marathon runner. "Running is a hoot!," Rector explains. "There is no doubt that running relieves stress." Rector runs with the OGE Running Team and has served as the president of the Oklahoma City Running Club.

When OGE retirees gather at the companywide Pioneer Club Meeting, they demonstrate a wide range of second careers. Some have included:

Retiree Judy Browning clowns it up with the Silver Foxes barbershop quartet at a Pioneer Club meeting.

- Zeb Bowles, picture framer.

- Judy Browning, entertainer.

- Robert Chester, volunteer at the Railroad Museum of Oklahoma.

- Neal DuBois, arts and crafts.

- Glynna Gunnell, author of *Sharing the Lite* cookbook.

- Joe Milsap, wood turning.

- Sondra Mount, beauty consultant.

- Emerson Pribble, volunteers at Cookson Hills Christian School.

- Ted Riddle, owner of the Homestead Bed and Breakfast.

- Ron Smithee, professional collector of American Indian artifacts.

- Eldon Waugh, beekeeper and operator of a honey business.

Retiree Jack Cox has participated in company-sponsored bowling events for more than forty years.

Left: Retired Enid Community Relations Manager Ralph Evans and his wife Beverly helped during the 1997 Enid franchise election. Here, they discuss the campaign with Enid resident Marie Hopson (right).

CHAPTER 11

OGE Energy Corp. at 100

I n February 2002, OGE Energy Corp. celebrated a century serving the people of Oklahoma and western Arkansas. If the company's members have learned a lesson in that time, it is that you can never "take things for granted." Any corporation must constantly look for ways to improve its relationship with customers, with others in the industry, and the efficiency with which it delivers service. At 100 years of age, OGE has developed a vision for the future.

As the new century and millennium dawned, the members and customers of OGE Energy Corp. paused and looked upon a community and the utility that serves it with deep, justifiable pride. They had withstood pressures and threats inconceivable from the vantage point of 1902 when the founders incorporated the company. The company successfully navigated the unique and changing utility landscape. OGE Energy had changed—but was stronger. "We've done a great job," says current Chairman, President, and CEO Steve Moore. "I try to celebrate [their commitment] every time I stand up in front of the employees— because they've done a very good job!"

The new age dawning started much like the old era—repeated storms, increased demand, and regulatory issues. "Looking back at the past year [2000], we had record storms in the summer, record storms in the winter, record peak demand for electricity in the summer, and peak demand for electricity in the winter. We had these big four operational events in 2000!" Moore said. In spite of OGE's challenges to meet increased customer demand, coping with emergencies, and dealing with multiple issues, the power continued to flow.

Left: CEO Steve Moore with members. Inset: OGE Energy Corp. advertisement designed to promote convergence.

A Solid Company with a Bright Future

Today, OGE is a financially stable, operationally successful company. In 2001, OGE Energy Corp. entered the *Fortune* 500 list of the nation's largest companies in terms of sales. Yet despite the distinction,

Enogex natural gas pipelines.

Below: Margaret White, customer support specialist, Shared Services.

OGE ranks among the smaller, regional energy producers and providers. And that is one of the components for the company's success. "We have a very unique set of assets," Moore continues. "We have an extensive electric operation, an extensive gas operation, and they lay right on top of each other. That's unique."

Another component of the OGE success story has been the company's willingness to take bold, often painful measures in order to maintain customer focus. "We're now growing the business for the first time in fifteen years," Moore explains. "We're hiring employees, reinvesting, building power plants and new substations. We're doing things we haven't done since the early 1980s in terms of growing our business."

That is primarily due to the hard work of members to change the company's culture. The end result has been a much more efficient organization.

Our Future Vision—Convergence

OGE has a strategy for the future. The twenty-first century will be a far distance in time and in operations from the Old West days in 1902 when Theodore Roosevelt was president of the United States.

OGE Energy's members have worked as a team to develop the vision for the future. The vision statement, "OGE Energy will be the converged, low-cost energy platform preferred by customers in our region," takes deregulation and *convergence* (pooled multiple sources of

continued on page 155

OGE's Current CEO

Steve Moore was happily driving a brand new Chevrolet and making an impressive $1,000 a month salary as assistant attorney general of the state of

Oklahoma when he got a telephone call that would change his life. That was in the spring of 1974. The call was from the Law Department of OG&E.

Steve Moore is an Oklahoma native, born in the western part of the state. Steve took degrees in business and law from the University of Oklahoma, and after a stint in the U.S. Army Reserve, took a job in the state attorney general's office in November 1971. His work was to represent the state environmental agencies, the Department of Agriculture, the Water Resources Board, the Air Quality Council, and others.

He got to know people from OGE Energy during various power plant application processes in the early 1970s. "I enjoyed public service very much," Moore remembers. "I found it very rewarding and thought I would pursue it as a long-term opportunity." But that career path took a turn when OGE's

Law Department made the fateful call with a job offer in 1974. He came on board as an OGE member, working with condemnation and land acquisition issues related to the building of the Sooner Power Plant.

As the years unfolded and the Carter administration passed the National Energy Act of 1978, Moore devoted virtually full time to governmental issues, particularly involving the changeover from gas- to coal-fired energy production. Successfully steering the company through the many hearings and applications, Moore eventually was given the job of manager of the Law Department (equivalent of general counsel) in 1984. Two years later, he became vice president of Law and Public Affairs, while at the same time taking a position as a company officer.

Steve worked closely with Jim Harlow during the extended periods of reorganization—especially the downsizing efforts of 1987 and 1994. By 1995, Jim Harlow was ready to step back and the logical choice was to place Steve in the president's chair, owing to his extensive knowledge of the legal and political parts of the utility industry.

Jim Harlow's unexpected death in 1996 propelled Steve Moore into the CEO and chairman roles—sooner than he would have expected. Yet Steve Moore has survived and flourished. Today he heads a company listed on the *Fortune* 500 list of America's largest companies. OGE serves more than seven hundred thousand customers and through Enogex operates one of the ten largest natural gas pipelines.

A phone call in 1974 made quite a difference, indeed.

OGE Energy Corp. Chairman, President and CEO Steve Moore paints the vision of convergence for the company's future.

Awards and Distinctions

Over the years, OGE Energy Corp. has received scores of prestigious awards from respected organizations. But during the past few years, there have been some very special and exceptional accomplishments for the members who make up OGE and its shareowners.

On January 13, 2000, the Edison Electric Institute presented OGE Energy with its distinguished Emergency Response Award in recognition of the company's incredible response to the outbreak of fifty-one tornadoes that swept through the area on May 3, 1999, wreaking havoc. "OGE's performance under dire natural circumstances is a model for electric utilities everywhere," said EEI President Thomas R. Kuhn in presenting the award. "They are to be congratulated for their sterling response on behalf of their customers."

In 2001, OGE Energy was presented the Emergency Response Award again for its restoration efforts during the Christmas 2000 ice storm and the 2001 Memorial Day windstorm.

On January 8, 2001, *Forbes Magazine* heralded OGE Energy for the second straight year in that publication's Platinum 400 list of America's best companies. Forbes describes the Platinum 400 as: "A list of big corporations that pass a stringent set of hurdles measuring both long- and short-term growth and profitability. Only about one in three of America's giant firms made the final cut."

OGE Energy Corp. joined the Fortune 500 list of the nation's largest companies in April 2001. At the same time, OGE's Sooner and Muskogee Power Plants were granted the Five-Star Award by Resource Data International, Inc. (RDI), the power-generation industry's leading independent consulting and research organization specializing in energy industry studies. The Five-Star Award rated Muskogee and Sooner in the top seven percent of all such plants in the nation on a basis of efficiency and competitiveness. RDI cited both facilities as attaining "the highest ranking achievable, signifying superior performance."

In October 1999, OGE was presented with the Dan J. Macer Environmental Award. Given by the University of Oklahoma College of Public Health, the award recognizes the company's efforts in increasing public awareness of environmental issues. The award cited OGE initiatives in the following areas:

- Support and participation in Oklahoma City's Ozone Air Alert Program.
- Sponsorship of City Shine '99, a metro Oklahoma City antilitter and environmental education campaign.
- Sponsorship of Cool Communities, promoting energy conservation through strategic tree planting.
- Sponsorship of Oklahoma Department of Environmental Quality's Hazardous Waste Collection Day.
- Support for environmental education in Oklahoma City's schools, providing materials and programs.
- Volunteer participation in the Environmental Protection Agency's sulfur hexafluoride emission reduction.
- Commitment to use low-sulfur coal.

energy) as a basis for future operations. Convergence simply defined means "to bring together." For the new century, OGE Energy brings together all assets and experience in electric power and natural gas to fuel industry and economic growth in Oklahoma, western Arkansas, and beyond.

OGE Energy's strategy is to be identified in the marketplace as the preferred energy provider—a growth strategy based on strong customer relationships.

Convergence begins where gas emerges from underground at the wellhead and ends at the electric outlet or gas burner. OGE Energy's job is to capture value at every step in between.

Four guiding principles have been fashioned in order for OGE to attain the proclaimed vision:

Right: The January 2002 ice storm was the worst in the company's history. More than 60 towns were affected in northeastern, central, and northwestern Oklahoma. Costs for the repairs are expected to top $100 million. Norris Carrier, lineman, Power Delivery, Sapulpa, works to restore service to customers in Crescent.

1st President:	George H. Wheeler	1902
2nd President:	A.H. Branch	1902–1903
3rd President:	Judge Charles B. Ames	1903–1904
4th President:	J. J. Henry	1904
5th President:	Dennis T. Flynn	1904
6th President:	Judge Charles B. Ames	1904–1910
7th President:	"Colonel" Henry M. Byllesby	1910–1924
8th President:	Arthur S. Huey	1924
9th President:	John J. O'Brien	1924–1931
10th President:	James F. "Jack" Owens	1931–1942
11th President:	George A. Davis	1942–1949
12th President:	Donald S. Kennedy	1949–1966
13th President:	Wayne A. Parker	1966–1973
14th President:	James G. Harlow Jr.	1973–1995
15th President:	Steven E. Moore	1995–present

OGE Energy's Honor Roll of Presidents

Steve Moore serves as Chairman, President and CEO. In OGE's history, only Donald S. Kennedy and James G. Harlow Jr. held those three posts simultaneously.

OG&E on the Cutting Edge of Cyberspace Customer Service

In September 2001, OGE unveiled yet another giant step on the road to total customer service. System Watch™, a Web page accessed through OGE's Web site at www.oge.com provides customers with real-time outage data. In what was believed to be the first such Internet access for a utility in the United States, System Watch™ enables customers to find the location of a power outage, number of customers affected, and information about how power is restored following damaging storms. The new service was a result of requests made by OG&E customers. Many customers can access the Internet using battery-operated laptops or can get the information from a remote location such as at work.

To help celebrate a century of service, this 9-foot birthday cake made of wood and trimmed with 100 candles was constructed to welcome members and guests to OGE Energy Corp.'s 100th birthday celebration on February 21, 2002, at the Civic Center Music Hall. Members attended a concert featuring entertainer Debbie Reynolds.

- Maintaining operational excellence.
- Pursuing disciplined growth.
- Developing new skills.
- Preparing for deregulation.

As the new face of OGE takes shape in the future years and decades, the company will continue to highlight the uniqueness of its electric and natural gas assets—pipelines and power lines virtually intertwined.

To spread the vision, OGE Energy Chairman of the Board, President and CEO Steve Moore and Executive Vice President and Chief Operating Officer Al Strecker have been seeking out and speaking with company members, giving the message of convergence and painting the vision of the company for the next century. The assets, and the good people who manage them, position OGE for a positive and strong future.

100 Years!

OGE Energy members and customers have experienced ten decades of reliable service. Very few people—and fewer companies—are around one hundred years after their birth. People—and companies—who are, attribute their longevity to their health.

OGE's health has always been its people. OGE members are also unassuming, relatively ego-less, and filled with a genuine desire to do the best for its customers.

The Oklahomans and Arkansans who form OGE today have inherited much from their determined, perhaps stubborn, risk-taking ancestors. For anyone to survive the weather, financial crises, and occasional disasters takes a special quality of confidence and pride. Those are the unique ingredients: confidence and pride. You'd have to have them to form a society here. You must have them to forge a new century in uncertain times. OGE Energy Corp. has confidence and pride. And its eyes are on the future. ■

The Meter—OGE's Voice since 1920

For eighty-two of OGE's one hundred years, the *Meter* has provided information and communications to OGE's members. Begun as the *Oklahoma Meter* on September 22, 1920, the publication was a typewritten newsletter—a format for the leadership team to communicate important events. It also was a society page for the many clubs within OGE. The *Meter* reported on personal accomplishments, births, deaths, marriages, vacations, "who caught the biggest fish," and similar human-interest topics.

Former President George A. Davis was the inaugural editor of the publication. That was understandable since Davis' expertise was public relations and marketing. Davis had done similar work for the H. M. Byllesby Company in Chicago, and was brought to Oklahoma City by OGE's Jack Owens.

Over the years, the *Meter* grew from a single page, typewritten, to mimeograph, to multiple typeset pages. Started as a weekly, the publication became bi-weekly, then monthly, and eventually quarterly over the years. At the same time, it has dramatically transformed from a mimeographed sheet complete with human and humorous typos, into a slick, highly professional, award-winning four-color publication, eagerly awaited by OGE members and retirees. The *Meter* has never failed to portray the human side of OGE—from the first issue until today, the publication has highlighted individuals' accomplishments, underscoring their contributions to the company as a whole.

Few companies can boast an uninterrupted house publication such as the *Meter*. Perhaps OGE members have come to take the publication for granted. Yet, the original vision of George Davis—of a publication to bring the OGE members closer together in their joint mission to serve customers—has served the company for eighty-two years.

Top: OGE Energy Corp. has headquartered Enogex at a modern office building located at 515 Central Park Drive in Oklahoma City.

Left: OGE headquarters building.

Centennial Members

Of all the people who have worked for OGE Energy Corp. in the utility's one hundred years of service, only three of record were born in the company's year of founding—1902.

Former OG&E President **Donald Kennedy** was born January 5, 1902, in Rushville, Indiana.

Albert Bogle, born February 17, 1902, hired on as a twenty-six-year-old member in March 1928. Bogle spent almost thirty-nine years with the company, retiring as Serviceman 1 in the Southern Division at Pauls Valley, Oklahoma, in March 1967. Bogle passed away February 15, 1999, two days short of his ninety-seventh birthday.

Louis Barnes was born on Christmas Eve 1902 and joined the company in June 1933. He retired as Supervisor A in community relations in Oklahoma City in March 1967. Barnes died on January 16, 1981, three weeks after his seventy-ninth birthday.

Company Logos Over the Years

OKLAHOMA GAS AND ELECTRIC COMPANY

An Oklahoma Institution • Established, Oklahoma Territory, 1902

OKLAHOMA GAS AND ELECTRIC COMPANY

Corporate Headquarters

101 North Robinson • Post Office Box 321 • Oklahoma City, Oklahoma 73101-0321 • 405-272-3000

OG&E's Plant Chronology

1902 • Robinson and Frisco Streets. The original power plant predated incorporation. It was the one and only power facility that used coal to generate as much as seven hundred kilowatts for street lighting and home use.

1909 • Noble Street. The Noble Street Generating Station was OG&E's first new plant. The facility used natural gas to produce electric power in its run at Southwest Third and Broadway, which lasted until 1959.

1923 • Byng Station. Acquired by OG&E in an expansion in 1923, Byng's former owners had built two power generators in 1916. OG&E added two more 6,000-kilowatt units in 1927. Byng eventually fell behind the times and was phased out and dismantled in 1976.

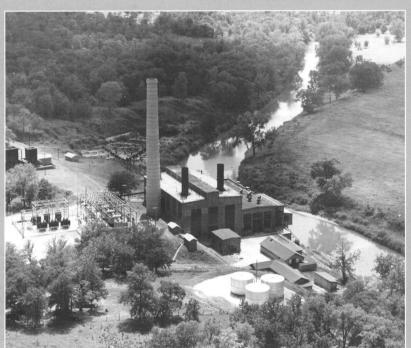

Byng

*1924 • Horseshoe Lake Station. One of OG&E's largest ventures, Horseshoe Lake added units one through three in 1924 through 1928, units four and five in 1947, unit six in 1958, unit seven (the world's first large combined-cycle power plant) in 1963, unit eight in 1969, and units nine and ten in 2000. Units one through five were retired in 1981.

*1924 • Muskogee Station. Muskogee started life as the Riverbank Station in 1924. Its name was changed to Muskogee in March 1972. It gained importance and distinction as additional units were added. Unit three was added in 1956, units four and five in 1977 and 1978, and unit six in 1984. Units one and two were retired in 1981. Muskogee generates power through coal as well as gas operations. Muskogee is the largest total-capacity power plant in Oklahoma.

1927 • Shattuck. In another acquisition, OG&E purchased this fuel-oil power generating plant whose original units were built in 1922. Subsequent expansions in 1927, 1929, 1947, and 1962 served customers' needs until the facility was taken offline and placed on standby status in 1976. The plant was demolished in the 1970s.

1928 • Belle Isle Station A. In 1928, OG&E purchased Belle Isle, the site of an amusement park and a power-generating station for interurban streetcar lines serving Oklahoma City, El Reno, Norman, and Guthrie. The streetcar line had built four power units to serve the lines, one dating from 1905, another from 1911, and two more in 1917. These were eventually demolished in 1960.

1929 • Osage Station. Started as the Lincoln Beerbower Plant named after a former OG&E plant manager. An additional unit was added in 1948, and the plant took on its present name in 1950. Osage closed in the late 1970s.

1930 • Belle Isle Station B. On the Belle Isle A. location, OG&E built four subsequent power-generating units. The first, a 30,000-kilowatt facility, was named originally the Arthur S. Huey Station after a former Byllesby and OG&E president who died in 1924. Three additional units were also built. Unit two was added in 1943, unit three (the first gas turbine in the United States to run a generator) in 1949, and unit four in 1952. The facility was retired in 1981 and demolished in the 1990s.

Osage

*1936 • Woodward. Originally built to serve Woodward and Shattuck. The first unit dates from 1922, with a second coming online in 1928. OG&E purchased the parent company in 1936 and built subsequent power generators in 1941, 1947, 1948, and 1963. Prior to its demolition in the 1970s, the gas turbine was moved to a location south of Woodward where it continues to function.

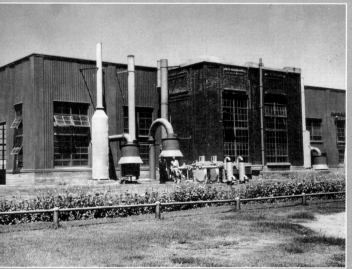

Woodward

*1950 • Mustang Station. Post–World War II power needs prompted the building of the largest plant in the OG&E system at the time. Additional installations that were placed online were unit 2 in 1951, unit 3 in 1955, unit 4 in 1959, and units 5A and 5B in 1971. Units 5A and 5B were relocated to Tinker Air Force Base in 1989.

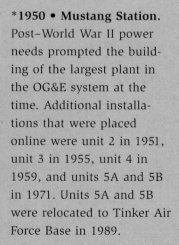

continued on page 162

OG&E's Plant Chronology continued

1953 • Arbuckle Station. OG&E's only outdoor power generation plant. The unit was put into long-term lay-up in 1987 with the intent to reactivate if needed to meet system demand. Arbuckle was retired in 2001.

*1963 • Enid Station. Enid has four gas-turbine power generators and is remotely operated from Sooner Station.

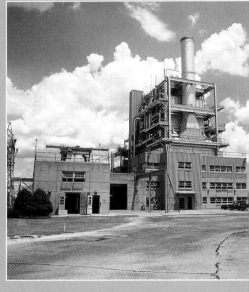

*1971 • Seminole Station. The largest plant built at the time, Seminole, near Konawa, was the last natural gas–fired steam plant to be built by OG&E. Unit two was added in 1972 and Unit 3 in 1975.

Arbuckle

*1979 • Sooner Station. The third and fourth coal-fired boiler in the OG&E system. They were installed in 1979 and in 1980. The plant is cooled by a man-made lake, which was designed for additional 3,500 megawatts of capacity. Sooner Lake has public recreational activities that include fishing and boating.

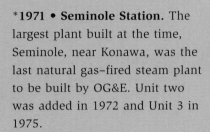

Enid

*1990 • Conoco Cogenerator. Installed to serve both steam-load for the refinery and electrical generation for the grid by using a mixture of high hydrogen content refinery gas mixed with natural gas as a fuel supply.

Denotes an active facility.

Seminole

OGE ENERGY CORP.

Board of Directors

Steven E. Moore
Chairman of the Board,
President and Chief
Executive Officer

Herbert H. Champlin[1,2]
President,
Champlin Exploration
Inc.
Enid, Oklahoma
*Chairman, Audit
Committee*

Luke R. Corbett[1,2]
Chairman and Chief
Executive Officer,
Kerr-McGee Corporation,
Oklahoma City

William E. Durrett[1,3]
Senior Chairman of the
Board,
American Fidelity
Corporation,
Oklahoma City

Martha W. Griffin[1,2]
Owner, Martha Griffin
White Enterprises,
Muskogee, Oklahoma
*Chairman, Nominating
Committee*

Hugh L. Hembree III[1,3]
Managing Partner,
Sugar Hill Partners
Fort Smith, Arkansas

Robert Kelley[1,3]
President,
Kellco Investments, Inc.,
Ardmore, Oklahoma

**Ronald H. White,
M.D.[1,2]**
President and Chief
Executive Officer,
Cardiology Inc.,
Oklahoma City

J. D. Williams[1,2]
Firm Founder
Williams and Jensen PC,
Washington, D.C.

Corporate Management

In addition to Steve Moore *(pictured above)*, who serves as OGE Energy Corp. Chairman, President and CEO, the OGE management team is comprised of the following officers as of January 1, 2002.

Al M. Strecker
Executive Vice
President, Chief
Operating Officer
OGE Energy Corp.,
OG&E Electric Services

James R. Hatfield
Senior Vice President,
Chief Financial Officer
OGE Energy Corp.,
OG&E Electric Services

Roger A. Farrell
President and Chief
Executive Officer
Enogex Inc.

David E. Garcia
Group President
OGE Energy Resources
Inc.

Jack T. Coffman
Senior Vice President
Power Supply
OG&E Electric Services

Melvin D. Bowen Jr.
Vice President
Power Delivery
OG&E Electric Services

Michael G. Davis
Vice President
Marketing & Customer
Care
OGE Energy Corp.,
OG&E Electric Services

Irma B. Elliott
Vice President and
Corporate Secretary
OGE Energy Corp.,
OG&E Electric Services

Steven R. Gerdes
Vice President
Shared Services
OGE Energy Corp.,
OG&E Electric Services

David J. Kurtz
Vice President,
Business Development
OGE Energy Corp.

Donald R. Rowlett
Vice President,
Controller
OGE Energy Corp.,
OG&E Electric Services

Eric B. Weekes
Treasurer
OGE Energy Corp.,
OG&E Electric Services

Don L. Young
Controller, Corporate
Audits
OGE Energy Corp.,
OG&E Electric Services

[1]Member of the Audit Committee
[2]Member of the Nominating Committee
[3]Member of the Compensation Committee

OGE Scrapbook

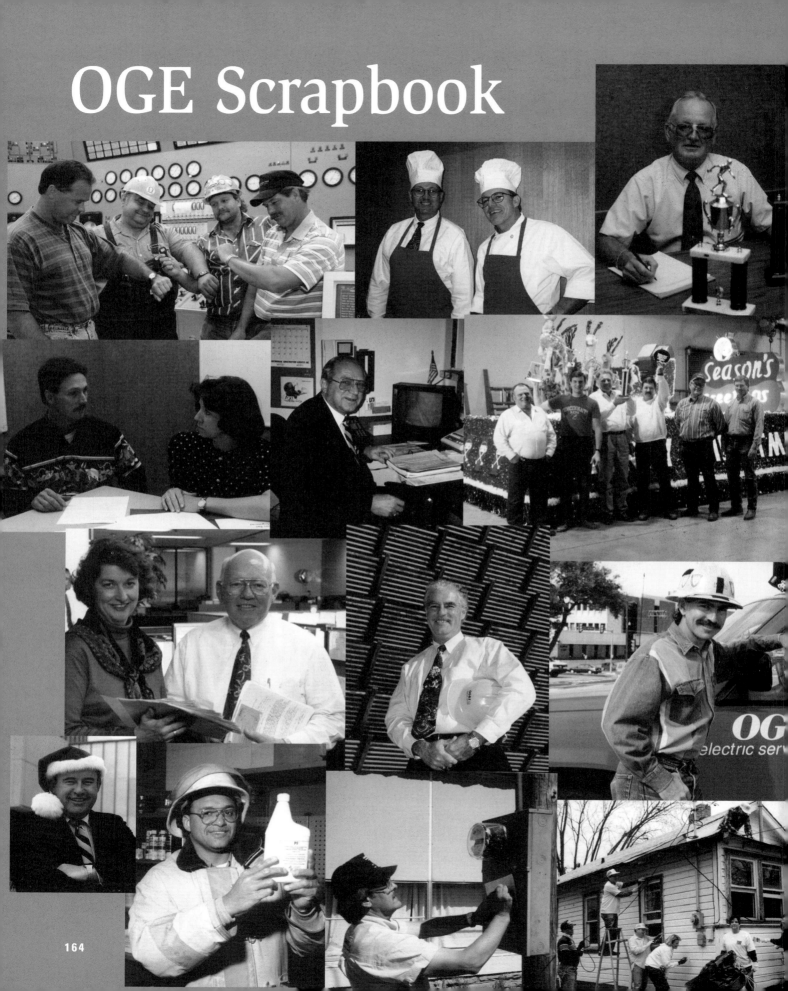

**OGE Energy Corp.
Active Members
as of
January 1, 2002**

Duplicate listings indicate
two people with the
same name.

• CORPORATE SERVICES

Adams, Kenny
Alford, Brian
Allison, Lisa
Alls, Linda
Anderson, Martin
Andrews, Coye
Anthony, Bob
Aucoin, Robbi
Baxter, Sheri
Beall, Melvin
Bell, Anita
Bennett, Beverly
Billington, Mendy
Bishop, Debra
Blundell, Brenda
Bowers, Steve
Boyer, Carolyn
Boyer, Terena
Branton, Tammi
Brockman, Carla
Bullard, Bill
Buller, James
Burgert, Laura
Burrows, Phil
Busch, Bill
Buxton, Leslie
Campbell, Ken
Cantrell, Scharon
Carr, Rhonda
Carson, Marcia
Carter, Deanna
Coachman, Jimmye
Collins, Geoffrey
Combs, Ward
County, Gloria
Cross, Terry
Curran, Theresa
Darby, Karen
Davenport, Cassie
Dedig, Kathleen
Douglas, Charles
Dukeman, Christina
Elliott, Irma
Elmore, Kevin
Ferrell, Richard
Ford, Jodie
Ford, Rob
Freeman, Kevin
French, Vivian
Fryar, Carol
Garber, Martin
Gay, Linda
Geurin, Bill
Gier, Mike
Goldschmidt, Diane
Goodner, Stephen
Gunesch, John, Jr.
Hall, Ben
Hall, Carri
Hamill, Richard
Hardebeck, Steve
Harkness, Susan
Hartley, Tim
Hartpence, Stephen
Hatfield, James
Heigle, Colette
Hellwege, Jan
Hennessy, Dale

Hill, Carol
Hill, Rick
Hollis, Charles
Howell, Leon C.
Huneryager, Gary
Hurley, Penny
Hutchinson, Brenda
Johnson, Karen
Johnson, Matt
Jones, Beverly
Jones, Craig
Jones, Teresa
Jweid, Bill
Kang, Kap S.
Keener, Janet
Keyser, Jeff
Kiespert, Sarah
Kilby, Don
Koenig, Robert
Kropp, Wendell
Kueter, Gary
Kurtz, David
Lampton-Jones, Emily
Lane, Sonny, III
Langston, Jesse
Lankford, Craig
Lashley, Anne
Lauderdale, Gary
Lawson, Steve
Laxton, Brian
Lewis, Gale
Lilburn, Linda
Mach, Laura
Maltby, Richard
McClellan, Debra
McCormack, James
McKellips, Shawna
McLelland, Russell
McMillen, Zollie, Jr.
Melrose, Robert
Milner, Sharon
Minnick, Madge
Mitchell, Dennis
Montgomery, C. D.
Moore, Steve
Morrison, Cheryl
Motley, Howard, Jr.
Neal, Edna
Nguyen, Van
Oliver, Karen
Patterson, Doug
Peters, Debbie
Phillips, Darlene
Phinney, Shirley
Pittenger, Steve
Place, Alan
Plog, Sabrina
Ponder, Dwight
Pound, Diane
Purvis, Molly
Raines, Jackie
Ramos, Betty
Ray, Kim
Reich, Richard
Renfrow, Paul
Rice, Rae
Roesch, Vickie
Ross, Rebecca
Rowlett, Donald
Sandefur, Norma
Saulters, Thomas
Sesock, John
Sexton, Robert
Shelton, Yvonne
Sheriff, Mike
Shoals, Linda
Shook, Nancy
Slama, Christy
Smelser, Kelly
Smith, Bob L.
Smith, Reggie
Smith, Leon, Jr.

Stewart, Robert D., Jr.
Strecker, Al
Streitmatter, Scott
Sutton, Venoral
Taylor, Jimmy
Tehauno, Glenn
Terry, Frankie
Tibbits, Millie
Tidwell, Todd
Tiffin, Don
Tippit, Richard
Tolbert, Shonna
Toler, Vanessa
Treat, Philip
Trent, Janet
Vance, Randy
Veitch, Greg
Vernon, Shelia
Walkingstick, Roger
Walters, Vikki
Ward, Twyla
Wasland, Sheila
Weaver, Brenda
Weekes, Eric
Wegner, Amy
White, Susie
Wilhelm, Walt
Wilkerson, Bill
Wilson, James
Wing, Rita
Wooden, Sandy
Wright, Mary
Wright, Tom
Wythe, Zeda
Yarbrough, Charlotte
Young, Don
Young, Michael

• ENOGEX

Abbott, Guy
Abbott, Michael
Abel, Eric
Adams, Leanna J.
Adams, Marla
Adler, Timothy
Alexander, Homer
Alfonso, Todd
Allen, Ike
Allen, Orval
Anquoe-Parnacher, Cheryl
Arnold, Mark
Ashlock, Cecil W., Jr.
Atkinson, Bobbi C.
Atkinson, James A.
Atkinson, Jerry L.
Atteberry, Johnny D.
Avila, Francisco O.
Awbrey, Stephen R.
Ballard, Barry
Barber, Angela
Barnes, Emily
Barrington, Kenneth R.
Bateman, Bernard A.
Bates, Bradley J.
Bates, John
Battles, Danny C.
Baxter, Gregory
Becker, Jay Lee
Bell, Ernest M.
Benham, Robert N.
Bergeson, Eldon
Bingham, Patty
Black, Josh
Blankenship, Gerry
Bledsoe, Stephanie
Bley, Lavern
Bobbitt, John
Bond, Vander E.
Bowen, Jerry
Bowermon, Marcia
Braden, Evelynn

Bradley, Mark
Branch, Donald R.
Bray, Randy
Breeding, Randy R.
Brewer, Timothy
Bridges, Jerry
Briscoe, Matthew
Brito, Alonzo
Broeker, Brian
Brooks, Kevin C.
Brown, Jerry W.
Bruce, Terri
Bunch, Lawrence N.
Burch, Clarence W., Jr.
Burrell, Jamie
Burrows, Dustin
Burrows, Kenny C.
Butler, Larry J.
Bybee, Monty W.
Bynog, Bobby
Callaway, Paul
Calvery, Robert
Calvillo, David E.
Cammack, Becky
Campbell, Kenneth P.
Canida, Marti O.
Cantrell, Linda
Care, Gina G.
Carpenter, Hollis
Carpenter, Lawrence D.
Carr, Kendal R.
Cauthron, Michael
Chambers, Tess
Chang, Wayne
Chaplin, Kenneth
Cheek, John R.
Childers, Sherry
Childers, Teresa
Chronister, Jerry
Clapp, Kerry
Clayton, Jeremy
Clem, Ryan
Cloud, Gary
Coats, Richard
Coble, Larry L.
Coffman, Joe
Colley, Aleathia
Collier, Chuck
Collins, Mark W.
Cook, J. D.
Cooper, John
Cooper, Les
Cortez, Bobby
Costley, David
Cottrell, Brooks
Crabtree, Shawn
Crowell, Michael E.
Culbertson, William C.
Culliver, Brian A.
Cummings, Jamie
Cummins, Karen
Curtis, Verlin
Davis, Martha
Davis, Paul
Davis, Tommy
Day, Ray
Deatherage, Joseph C.
DeBose, Daniel
Deckard, Benay
Dedmon, H. C.
Dedmon, Jason
Deleon, Ramiro A.
DeLuca, Brian
Dennis, Michael
Denton, Connie
Deviney, Charles L., Jr.
Dickason, Nolan
Dickson, Harry P., III
Dobbs, Dallas
Dobbs, Tracie
Doerr, Robert
Dorman, Danny P.

Dove, Alan
Dow, Mary B.
Driskill, Gary L.
Drosselmeyer, David
Dubois, Jeannie
Dudley, Keith
Dunbar, Dianne
Eddlemon, Jimmy
Elliott, Judy C.
Ellis, Kevin
Ellis, Raymond
Embery, Jimmy L.
Esmon, Keith
Esparza, Eleazar
Estep, Michael
Eveld, Stanley
Evett, Stacy
Ewing, Lyric
Farrell, Roger
Farris, Roy
Farrow, Dean
Fergason, Marc
Ferguson, Delbert
Fisk, Darrell K.
Fixico, Stanley
Floeter, Tena
Flynn, Richard
Ford, Sue
Fort, Bill
Foster, David E.
Fox, Ronald D.
Frachiseur, Billy D.
Franklin, Paul D.
Frederick, James M.
Freeby, Robert C.
Freeman, Roger
Frie, Bret
Friesen, Chris A.
Fulton, Daniel
Gandy, Greg
Garcia, Thomas
Garner, Eddie R.
Garza, Jose
Garza, Luis
Gernhart, Earl D.
Gilmore, Charles, Jr.
Godwin, Dwayne
Goodson, Jeffrey
Gordon, Harold G.
Gorshing, Larry A.
Gradle, Michael
Gravens, Cheryl
Gray, Keenan
Green, Brian
Green, Dean A.
Green, Paul
Greenway, William D.
Gregg, Diann
Griffin, Bruce
Gronski, Sadie
Guinn, Tom
Haack, Timothy
Hagius, Frederick E.
Hall, Frederick C., Jr.
Halsted, Stephen
Hamman, Timothy C.
Hammons, Charles G.
Hamons, Carlisle L.
Hampton, Darrell D.
Hanes, Steve
Hankins, Jane
Hanson, Jeff
Hardnack, Thomas
Hargrove, Donna
Harper, Cytha L.
Harrell, David
Harrell, Grady
Harris, Danny
Harris, Steve
Harris, Terry L.
Harrison, Brad
Hart, James M.

Haugen, Chris
Haught, Marsha L.
Hawkins, Susan
Haydon, Michael
Hayes, Elaine
Hayes, Orville E.
Hayes, Joseph, Jr.
Haynes, Joe
Hearn, Stephen A.
Hedrick, Bruce
Hefner, Adam B.
Helton, Garland R.
Henderson, Steve
Henderson, Steven G.
Henry, Howard C., Jr.
Herrara, Nick, Jr.
Herring, Nita
Hickerson, Eddie L.
Hicks, Michael J.
Hicks, Tony
Higginbottom, Donna
Hill, David R.
Hill, James
Hill, Ricky
Hodges, Cecil K.
Holley, Ricky
Holman, Sally
Holmes, David
Hooker, Craig
Horn, Trish
Houck, Eugene
Hough, Alan
Howey, Richard
Hubbard, Jimmy
Hughes, Bill
Hull, Amelia
Hulsey, John
Hunter, Bret
Huser, Karen
Ingle, Wade
Inman, Brian
Jackson, Delbert E.
Jenkins, Rickie L.
Johnson, Buford M.
Johnson, Linda
Johnson, Stephen G.
Johnston, Danny
Jones, Kenneth R.
Kahler, Gary R.
Kauk, Dennis K.
Kauk, Mitchell K.
Kelley, Clinton F.
Kelley, Leah
Kelly, Darrell T.
Kelso, Darcie
Kenneda, Wyly
Kennedy, Willis G.
Kennedy, Raymond, Jr.
Kent, Gary
Kerr, Richard E.
Kerrigan, David
Keyes, Dennis
Kilhoffer, Kevin L.
King, Alvin
King, Kenneth
King, Kenneth
King, Michael
Kitchens, Richard
Klein, Ronald
Knight, Rodney
Knoll, David
Koch, John
Korrect, Vickie
Kothe, Ronald L.
Kowalczik, Peter
Kroeker, Rick
Lawrence, Dennis K.
Lawson, James
Lawson, Kenneth W.
Lawson, Terry L.
Leedy, Ken
Leftwich, Curtis

Leger, Jean, Jr.
Legg, Kim
Lemley, Brooke
Lemons, Donald R.
Lewinski, Amarie
Lewis, Carol J.
Lewis, Steve
Lilly, Ted
Locke, William, Jr.
Loftis, Eric
Loyd, Kendall
Luper, Allan
Maas, Lynn
Marable, Lee A.
Margerum, Roger
Marquez, Robert
Marshall, Darrell
Martin, Robert
McAlester, John
McAnaugh, Doug
McCathern, Farron
McCroskey, Mary
McCullar, Boyd L.
McDaniel, Daniel
McDaniel, Mark
McDonald, Lollie
McElfresh, Albert
McGovern, Donald
McGugan, Mark
McInnerney, Brian
McIntyre, Michael
McKinney, Bill
McMillin, Eugene
McRae, Danny
Meador, David
Miller, Jill
Miller, Kirk
Miller, Steven
Miller, Tony
Mills, Larry
Mills, Rick
Mills, Stephen
Mink, Monty W.
Mitchell, Keith
Mitchum, Robert
Molinaro, Donald M.
Molone, Matthew
Moore, Emily
Moore, Maria
Morgal, Michael
Morris, Steven
Morse, Jerry
Morton, Michael
Murch, John
Murray, Vowell
Myers, Larry D.
Nave, Felix
Neal, Gary D.
Nealis, Tom
Needham, Robert Kelly
Neese, Mark
Neves, Toby
Newberry, Michael
Newer, Kenneth
Nimmo, Dusty
Noble, Candace
Noblett, Elizabeth
Noey, Melvin
Norman, Michaelle
Norman, R. C.
Nowka, Janice
Ocker, Michael
Oglesby, Monty
Orahood, Shery L.
Osborn, Jeffrey
Pack, Jacob
Palladino, Lori
Parker, Dale
Partridge, Jerry
Payne, Richard
Pease, Tracy A.
Peck, Dwight

Peel, Earl W.
Perry, Timothy
Perry, Todd K.
Peterson, Mark
Pettit, David P.
Phillips, Terry
Pierce, Wiley
Pierro, Kathie
Pike, Glen
Pittenger, Shannon
Pitts, Larry
Poindexter, Donald L.
Post, Vernon L.
Pounds, Billy J.
Powell, Clark
Pritchett, Randal
Querbach, Larry
Ramey, Dennis J.
Ramsdell, Gary
Ramsey, Ed
Ramsey, Michael D.
Ramsey, Ricky W.
Randolph, Patricia
Rangel, Sandra
Reagan, Michael R.
Reed, Michael
Reed, Thomas
Reichert, Deborah
Reynolds, Jason D.
Rhodes, Ruth
Richards, Jerry D.
Richardson, Jimmie
Richardson, Jon
Ricker, Jason
Riley, Hugh
Rizzo, Nakita
Roberts, Harold L.
Roberts, Toby
Rockett, Joey D.
Rodgers, Virgil
Roe, Michael
Roewe, David A.
Romeiser, Tim
Roper, Jamie A.
Russell, Mark
Russell, Rockne A.
Rutherford, Paula
Rutz, Samuel
Ryan, Thomas D.
Sadler, Ronald L.
Sanders, Jeffery
Sawyer, Bart
Sawyer, Ronald
Saxon, Larry
Schack, Bernard, Jr.
Scherr, Jerome J.
Schmidt, Linda
Schulz, Kervin L.
Scott, ShawnTrell
Seeley, Bobby L.
Seeley, Debbie
Sexton, Tommy
Sherril, Marcus A.
Shilling, Jerry
Shoemake, Carol
Shoestock, Anne
Simpson, Timothy
Sinor, David L.
Sipe, Rick
Sisson, Robert J.
Smith, Patrick
Snider, Mike E.
Soapes, Christina
Sodders, Phillip R.
Soell, Preston
Southard, Dennis
Sperling, Eric
Spicer, Michael
Springer, Cathy
Sproull, Mark J.
Spruill, Mark
Stamper, Billy R.

Staton, Timothy W.
Stevens, Donald L.
Stewart, Charles W.
Stewart, Danny L.
Stockman, Harvey
Stout, Lynn
Strain, Terry
Strawn, Larry
Struck, Jimmy
Stubbs, Brent A.
Suggs, Johnny
Swadley, Jon
Swim, Diane
Swindle, Kim E.
Swisher, Rod
Tanner, John
Tarin, Lupe
Taron, Diane
Tate, Terry
Taylor, James
Taylor, Richard
Taylor, Shirley.
Thionnet, Kent D.
Thompson, Deborah
Thompson, Jeremy
Tidball, Gary
Tiffee, Colby
Tillman-Sanders, Sharon
Todd, Sherri
Trammell, Jimmie D., Jr.
Traylor, Heath
Trevino, Pat
Turney, David
Van Huss, Phillip
Vaughan, Freddie L.
Venable, Rodney E.
Wahl, David W.
Walker, Michael L.
Walker, Robert
Wallace, Henry
Wallace, Penny
Walters, Michael
Walton, Tammi
Walz, Albert F.
Wanzer, Ramona
Warren, James
Warren, Shannon
Watkins, Brad
Wears, Robert L.
Weber, James
Webster, Don
Welcher, Terry
West, Gail
Whitaker, Gary
Whitley, Ben
Whitson, Lonnie D.
Wiedemann, Hal
Wilcox, George
Wilkinson, Kent
Williams, Lawrence T.
Williams, Mark K.
Williams, Robert G.
Williams, Roger
Williams, Tyson
Wilson, Charles
Wilson, Clifford
Wilson, David W.
Wilson, Kent
Wilson, Richard
Wilson, Stanley
Winlock, Stuart
Wint, David
Winters, Mike N.
Wood, Pamela
Wood, Ricky K.
Woodard, Rickey O.
Workman, Sean
York, Beckie
Yother, Robert O.
Young, Frank E.
Young, Wilburn
Youngblood, John

Zeiler, Freddie L

• ENERGY RESOURCES

Adams, Kerri
Annesley, Thomas M.
Anthony, Darrell
Arnold, Terri
Babbit, Kara
Baskett, Josh
Batt, Alan J.
Botsford, Bill
Brooks, Margaret
Brown, Tracy
Callaway, Doug
Cheatham, Kent
Dean, Susan
Diamond, Kenneth
Ederer, Ashley
Eldridge, Michael
Ensminger, Lance, III
Fash-Larsen, Beki
Gajewski, Martin
Garcia, David E.
Geiger, Lori
Gencheva, Daniela
Goodner, Erica
Gould, Holli
Green, John
Harbert, Kirk
Hays, Charlie
Henline, Kathryn
Henry, W. Craig
Jackson, Gary V.
Karr-ake, Kathryn E.
Kisling, Cynthia
Labadie, Jay
Lilly, Steve
Lindsay, James
Liszewski, Pete
Marolt, Cindy
Maynard, Marvena
Mercer, Donna
Moore, Joyce
Murphey, Patrick
Peace, Jerry
Prange, Sarah
Roll, John
Ross, Spencer
Russell, Joe
Sandusky, Danielle
Schurman, Rankin, II
Scouten, Robert
Shults, John W.
Stands, Steve
Swad, Tony
Tabbert, Leah
Walworth, Charles
Watson, Cary
Watson, Susan
Weatherford, Mike
Wilkes, Brandon
Wylie, William

• MARKETING AND CUSTOMER CARE

Adams, Melvonda
Adkins, Linda
Aldridge, Terry
Allen, Dale
Anderson, Loretta
Anderson, Rosalie
Badger, David
Bailey, Edward
Baird, Brandon
Bakeman, Julia
Banks, Veronica
Barker, Jerry
BarkerMiller, William
Barnes, Mark
Barnett, Anthony

Barnett, Dennis
Bartholomew, Philip
Basco, Michelle
Beach, Julie
Beam, Bruce
Beamon, Sherry
Beavers, Charles
Bell, J. P.
Bevers, Liz
Bieger, Joe
Black, Josh
Blair, Robert
Blanco, Ramon, Jr.
Blanton, Danny
Boevers, Chester
Bohrofen, Mike
Bolz, Janice
Bondoni, Ruth
Boone, Daniel
Booth, Theresa
Booze, Dorothy
Boren, Jeff
Boyd, Scott
Bradley, Kimberly
Bradley, Shawn
Bramlett, Keith
Bratcher, Brent
Brendle, Chuck
Breshears, Bruce
Britten, Neil
Brock, Lora
Brown, Billy
Brown, Dianna
Brown, Janice
Brown, Paulette
Bruehl, Paul
Bryant, Christy
Buchanan, Rodney
Buchanan, Steven
Bullard, Michael
Burden, Rodney
Burdick, Jeremiaha
Burks, Stephen
Byrd, John
Byrn, Max
Caldwell, James
Calvert, Mark
Campbell, Jimmie
Cantrell, Kimberly
Cantrell, Lowell
Cantwell, Mike
Carrick, Robert
Carter, Janet
Casey, Mary Jane
Cash, Gwin
Casteel, Janice
Cavnar, Cayce
Chaffin, Johnna
Chaffin, Ruth Ann
Challis, Elizabeth
Chambers, Randy
Chaplin, Tim
Chapman, Steve
Chappel, James
Chelf, Cody
Childs, Twila
Clack, David
Clark, Jason
Clark, Marilyn
Clark-Woody, Ragina
Clay, Kathryn
Clements, Richard
Clonts, Kelly
Cobb, Pamela
Coburn, Thomas
Cochran, Lisa
Coleman, Keisha
Collins, Krista
Compassi, Janie
Conners, Mark
Cooke, Linda
Cooper, Ronald

Cornelison, Richard
Cothran, Charles
Couch, Betty
Cowley, Troy
Cox, Matt
Coyner, Ronald
Craig, Dana
Cranfield, Carl
Creek, Tonja
Creel, Tim
Crooks, Jeff
Crowley, Rick
Crumley, Raymond
Davenport, Joyce
Davidson, Cheri
Davis, Lois
Davis, Mike
Davis, Janet
Davis, John, Jr.
Davis, Mekea
Davis, William
Deffenbaugh, D. L.
DeGraffenreid, Angela
DeGraffenreid, Deborah
Dennis, Bill
Dew, Melissa
Dickerson, Bruce
Dilbeck, Deborah
Dillier, Ardie
Dillon, Carolyn
Dixon, Keith
Dobbins, Kaydenzia
Douglas, Rebecca
Dragoo, John
Drake, Shane
Droke, Brenda
Dunlap, Misty
Dunn, Marion
Dunn, Nancy
Durbin, Phyllis
Dyer, Phyllis
Edwards, George
English, Chris
Epley, Katherine
Epperson, Sheryl
Escalante, Kevin
Estes, Ronald
Evans, Monaco
Ewing, Shelia
Ezell, Ronnie
Fauchier, Jimmy
Fields, Clyde
Filippo, Sheri
Filson Leslie, Jr.
Fisk, Josh
Fite, Ladonna
Fitzgerald, Martin
Fluke, Daryl
Flynn, Joseph
Foldvary, Michael
Foster, Craig
Foster, Kelly
Fox, Donald
France, George, IV
French, Jessica
Frisby, Mike
Fryar, Gene
Fugate, Tim
Gabriel, Stephanie
Gammon, William
Gibbs, Bobby
Goins, Clyde
Graham, Melanie
Grant, Kenneth
Greb, Ted
Green, Robin
Greenwood, Jerry
Gros, Dennis, II
Groves, Steven
Gurkowski, Jody
Guthrie, DeAnna
Hall, M. T.

Hall, Ertel, III
Hamilton, Patricia
Harkins, Jimmy
Harrell, Judith
Harris, J. Kent
Harris, James
Harris, Scott
Hartman, Susy
Harvey-Tuley, Sherry
Hawkins, Larry
Hayden, LaShonna
Haynes, Faye
Hays, Harold
Heartsill, Robert
Heimer, Peggy
Helton, James
Helton, Mike
Hensley, Bob
Hensley, Marsha
Hensley, Roger
Henson, Ann
Hickey, Stefanie
Hiebsch, Stephen
Higginbottom, Ralph
Hill, Michael
Hill, Shawn
Hill, William
Hirzel, Delores
Hodge, Dustin
Hodges, Robert, III
Holcomb, Brian
Holder, Victor
Hooper, Neil
Hoover, Billie
Horton, Debra
House, Marcellus
Howard, Gary
Huffman, Richard
Hull, Mike
Hunsaker, Floyd
Inman, Chad
Ives, Don
Jackson, Kevin
James, Rickey
Jenkins, Brian
Johnson, Amy
Johnson, Jarod
Johnson, John
Johnson, Natasha
Johnson, Sharon
Johnson, Tommy
Jones, Darren
Jones, Jay
Jones, Jennifer
Jones, Jon
Jones, Marilyn
Jones, Randy
Jones, Santon
Kardokus, Stephen
Kearns, Stan
Kelly, Pat
Kelly, Harold, II
Kerr, Kenny
Kimbrough, M. D.
Kinimaka, Deanne
Koch, Cynthia
Koegel, Eric
Koehn, Jeff
Koons, John
Laclair, Betty
Lacour, Cynthia
Lagaly, Michael
Langley, Sarah
Langston, Susan
Langwell, Darrell
Lanier, Darrel
Lanquist, Joeda
Lau, John
Lee, Ginger
Lemen, Jeff
Lemmings, Brien
Lewis, Debbie

Lewis, Pat
Lewis, Randy
Liddell, Luther
Ligon, Larry
Limas, Betty
Little, Franklin
Little, John
Littleton, Roy
Long, Michael
Love, D'
Lovett, Morris
Lowe, Keith
Loyd, M. V.
Ludwig, Bryan
Lyon, Tim
Malaska, Richard
Marchbanks, Gary
Marker, Earl
Martin, Patricia
Mason, Sheila
Matthews, LaShunda
Mauldin, Danny
Maurelli, Elizabeth
Maxwell, Danny
Maxwell, Darrell
Maxwell, Kevin
Maynard, Maggie
McCarrell, Nakia
McCown, Rick
McCurdy, Tom
McCurry, Brenda
McElwee, Terence
McGlon, Detra
McGowen, Joe
McIntire, Debra
McKinney, Dahl
Medaris, William
Meeh, John
Mester, Paula
Meyers, Chris
Mickey, Ramone
Mitchell, Chuck
Mitchell, Mike
Mitchell, Terrycia V.
Mohon, Angelia
Moon, Linda
Moore, Jack
Moore, Michael
Moore, Sheryl
Morris, Charles
Morris, Stevie
Mortenson, Kathy
Moss, Debra
Mullens, Jerry
Myers, Thomas
Myricks, Timothy
Nelson, Byron, Jr.
Nero, Gregory
Newberry, Christi
Newcombe, Mike
Nickel, Lourdes
Norman, Renee
Norton, Tammy
Owen, Dale
Paige, Edward
Pangborn, Rita
Parker, Diane
Parker, Nancy G.
Patmon, Minnie
Patton, Steve
Peery, Donna
Permetter, John, Jr.
Perry, Kady
Phillips, Amie
Pickens, Clarence
Pickett, Kim
Pickle, Virginia
Pilgrim, Jan
Platt, Cori
Plowman, Charles
Plunkett, Janice
Pollard, Donna

Poole, Buz, Jr.
Pospiech, Shannon
Prabhakara, G. R.
Puffer, Brandon
Quenzer, Kenneth
Rackley, Colton
Ratley, Rob
Reed, Barbara
Reed, Tina
Reeves, Ricky
Reynolds, Robert
Rich, Douglas
Richards, Gary
Richardson, Vicki
Rickey, David
Rinehart, Rickey
Rivera, Eduardo
Roach, Cynthia
Roberts, Janice
Roberts, Warren
Robertson, Jimmy
Robertson, Tommy D.,
   Sr.
Robinson, Glenn
Rogers, Brian
Rogers, Dorthy
Rogers, Otis, Jr.
Rogers, Rhett
Rogers, Scott
Romines, Stacy
Rosales, Darrell
Ross, Kenneth
Routh, Brian
Rozzell, Sandra
Ruby, Michael
Rucker, William
Rupert, Seth
Rutledge, Mary Ann
Ruyle, David
Ryan, David
Ryan, Vickie
Samuels, Larry
Sanders, Reginald
Santelmann, Steven
Schaper, Carol
Schritter, Sue
Schroeder, Ken, Jr.
Schroyer, Richard
Schwalbach, Brandon
Schwartz, Shellie
Schwartz, W. Kendal
Scott, Peggy
Scott, Rodney
Scribner, Bill
Seiden, Theresa
Semien, Phillip, II
Senter, Margaret
Seward, Roland
Sexton, David, Jr.
Shank, Aaron
Sharum, Larry, Jr.
Shaw, LaVonna
Shaw, Rusty
Shedeck, M. Milo
Shelton, Patrick
Sherrill, Robert
Shetley, Marsha
Shields, Donna
Silvey, Bruce
Simmons, Tony
Simon, J. Thomas
Simpson, D. C.
Singleton, Nakisha
Singley, Lisa A.
Skinner, Richard
Slaughter, Tena
Smith, Bob
Smith, Debra
Smith, Deborah
Smith, Dennis
Smith, Gary
Smith, Larry

Smith, Lindell
Smith, Michael
Smith, Rayne
Smith, Richard
Smoot, Renee
Sparks, K. W.
Spaulding, Jennifer
Springer, Anthony
Stanfield, Cathy
Starr, Portia
Steele, Debbie
Stefanick, Jack
Stejskal, Dusty
Stengle, Jim
Stevens, Alvest
Stevens, Danielle
Stevenson, Angela
Stewart, Nathan
Stone, Jason
Stover, Bart
Stuecken, Teri
Sullivan, Steven
Sweazy, Jill
Talley, S. Bertram
Taylor-Lawson, Alvett
Terry, David
Thomas, Ira
Thompson, B. J.
Thompson, Carolyn
Thompson, Lawanda
Todd, Sandy
Tolbert, Mike
Tolbert, Teri
Townsend, John
Townsend, Ruth Ann
Tran, Ty
Traywicks, Schnelle
Turner, Dewayne
Turtle, Jaycient
Underwood, Bill
Valero, Jonnie
Wade, Stephen
Walkabout, Nancy
Walker, Crystal
Walker, Jeremiah
Walker, Kent
Walker, Lee Ann
Walker, Wayne
Wallace, Terry
Wallingford, Rex
Walters, Monroe
Walters, Terri
Walton, Gerald
Ware, Marilyn
Warg, David
Warren, Randall
Watkins, Vincent
Weekley, Patricia
Weeks, Bill
Weigl, Paul, Jr.
Welch, James
Welch, Jerry
Wells, Willie, Jr.
Wheeler, Wilma
White, Connie
White, Glenn
White, Howard
White, William
Whitley, Raymond, Jr.
Whitlock, Brian
Wichert, Terry
Williams, Darrell
Williams, David
Williams, Eddie
Williams, Michael
Williams, Scott
Willis, Tommy
Wilson, J. V.
Wise, Jenifer
Wolff, Thomas
Wood, Doug
Wood, Scott

Woodberry, Staci
Woodrow, Kenneth
Woods, Jody
Woods, LaTonia
Woodward, T. L., Jr.
Worley, Donny
Wright, Sharron
Wright, Raymond, Jr.
Wunderlich, Mark
Wynd, Anthony
Yellowfish, Lisa
Young, Sherond

• POWER DELIVERY

Abel, Paul
Adams, Jeff
Adams, Phillip
Adams, Ryan
Adams, Wayne
Aebi, Steve
Albright, Bob, Jr.
Alcorn, Connie
Alexander, David
Alexander, Elaine
Allen, David
Allen, Jesse
Allensworth, Bill
Allred, James
Alls, Carl
Ames, Rena
Ammer, V. R.
Anderson, Bob
Anderson, Ike
Anderson, Kenneth
Antwine, Willie, Jr.
Apple, Phil
Archibald, Karen
Arevalo, Hermes
Armenta, Connie
Arpoika, Kathy
Asche, Adam
Ashford, Dewayne
Atchley, Billy
Autry, Marvin
Avant, Curt
Ayers, Mary
Bacon, Judy
Baird, Tom
Baker, Larry
Baldwin, Fran
Baldwin, Ray
Baldwin, Rusty
Bales, Kathal
Ballard, Sidney
Barnard, Joe
Barnes, Ricky
Barry, Prentis
Bass, Duane, Jr.
Bassett, John
Batchelder, Rick
Baxter, Joyce
Baxter, Leo
Beardmore, Steve
Beardslee, Bobby
Beaudoin, Dean
Bechtel, G. Russell
Beck, John
Becker, Bill
Beesley, Gregory
Beesley, James
Bell, Jeff
Berg, Rick
Bert, Chebon
Biggs, Kenneth
Bigpond, Gregory
Billinger, Ken
Billingsley, Jay
Billins, Bill
Bilyeu, Carl
Birdsong, Jim
Bishop, Dale

Blakley, Jim
Blanchet, Richard
Blanden, Randall
Bly, Donald, Jr.
Bogun, Tom
Bollinger, Paul
Bolton, Scott
Bond, Danny
Borges, Roger
Botts, Ricky
Bowen, Melvin, Jr.
Bowman, Donnie
Bowser, Gary
Boyd, Sammy
Bracken, Bobby
Bradley, Freddie
Brakebill, Rick
Branch, Timothy
Brashears, Greg
Brautigan, L. B.
Breger, Leslie
Bridges, Chad
Bridges, Charles
Bristol, Chris
Bristow, Pat
Bristow, Ronnie
Brooks, Greg
Brown, Gail
Brown, Greg
Brown, Jim
Brown, John
Brown, Les
Brown, Winford, Jr.
Browne, Chris
Browning, William, Jr.
Broyles, Chris
Bruch, Denise
Bryan, Celia
Buckles, Dale
Burcham, Steve
Burns, John
Burns, Zeke, Jr.
Burris, Jim
Burris, Robert
Butler, Dennis
Butler, Terry, Jr.
Callaway, C. W.
Calvert, Steve
Canada, Billy
Canady, Benjamin, Jr.
Cardwell, Gary
Carey, Adam
Carlisle, Lynn
Carlon, Lonnie
Carlton, Damon
Carpenter, James
Carrier, Norris
Carroll, Robert
Carter, Jimmy
Carter, T. E.
Carter, Timothy C.
Cartwright, Jeff
Case, Bob
Caskey, Steve
Caughern, Dwain
Chambers, Lonnie
Chandler, Rick
Chapple, Carl
Chapples, Holly
Charboneau, Keith
Chartney, Glenn
Chavez, Max
Cherry, Louis
Childers, Steven
Christian, Michael
Chronister, Chris
Ciupak, Don
Claypole, Joe
Clemmer, J. C.
Clifton, Dewayne
Clifton, Michael
Clubb, Kenneth

Coats, Larry
Cobb, Phillip
Coffey, Danny
Cogdill, Mike
Coker, Gale
Coleman, Michael
Combs, Jimmy
Comes, Dale
Compton, H. Wade
Compton, Stan
Conallis, Vance
Conley, Deon
Conner, Jason
Conner, John
Conrad, Acie
Conrad, Kenneth
Conrady, Mark
Cook, Gary
Cook, Jerry
Cookson, Larry
Coomer, Janssen
Cope, Debbie
Copeland, Dwight
Copeland, Gary
Couron, John
Covel, Gary
Cox, Rufus
Cox, Theressa
Coy, Linda
Crabb, Larry
Craig, Johnny
Craine, Charles
Crawford, Calvin
Creasey, Wes, Jr.
Creek, Victor
Crissup, Phil
Crocker, Bobby
Crowley, James
Crutchfield, Betty
Cue, Donnie
Cummins, Craig
Cummins, Mark
Cunningham, John
Curtis, Lee
Daly, John
Daniel, Curtis
Darrow, Harold
Davis, Charlotte
Davis, J. David
Davis, Leon
Davis, Tim
Davis, James, Jr.
Davis, James H., Jr.
Day, Gary
Day, Peter
Dean, Philip
Deason, Terry
Declark, Robert, Jr.
DeLano, Richard
Delashaw, Larry
Deshazo, William
Dickens, David
Dill, Steve
Dinwiddie, Keith
Dixon, J. Mark
Dobbs, Ben
Dobrinski, Tim
Dobson, Diana
Dockins, Carol
Dodson, G. Dwain
Drittler, Larry
Duke, Mike
Dumas, Tommy
Dunbar, Elaine
Earles, David
Eary, David
Eastwood, James
Ebert, Jerry
Ebert, Tommy
Echard, Stephen
Edwards, Eugene
Edwards, Melanie

Eichholz, Elden
Eisert, Randy
Ellard, Jon
Elliott, David
Elliott, Gary
Elliott, Tommy
English, D. L.
Epps, Debra
Ernst, Everett, Jr.
Eskew, Jim
Eubanks, Ron
Eubanks, Bill, Jr.
Evans, G. Dave
Evans, James
Evans, Stan
Ewing, Arnold
Fairbrother, Alan
Fant, Tracy
Faries, Bobby
Feero, Bryan
Finley, Christopher
Fisher, Jerry
Flewelling, John
Floyd, Steven
Foote, Michael
Ford, Tim
Ford, L. Allen, Jr.
Foster, Randy
Foster, Starla
Fox, David
Fox, Mike
Francis, Jay
Frazier, Jerry
Fried, Kevin
Friend, Rauk
Frizzell, Danny
Fugate, Gary
Fuller, Darrell
Fuller, P. J.
Gammel, Ronald
Gardner, Bill
Gardner, Kirby
Garner, Jack
Garner, Monty
Garren, Pete
Garrett, Craig
Garrett, Terry
Garrison, Dave W.
Garrison, J. Delbert
Gay, Richmond
Genow, Steven
George, Fred, Jr.
Gevaza, Mike
Gibbs, Robert
Gibson, Dale
Gilbert, Larry
Gilbert, Randy, Jr.
Gillion, Jerry
Gillispie, Greg
Gleim, Jeffrey
Glennie, Lawrence
Goad, Michael
Godwin, Daniel
Goeke, Michael
Golden, William
Goodner, Karen
Gordon, Steve
Gose, Ronald
Gotcher, Leroy
Gottschalk, Glenn
Gottshall, Robert
Grady, Reba
Graham, Kevin
Grandstaff, Robert
Green, Bret
Green, Richard
Green, Robert
Greenroyd, Rick
Greer, Harry
Gregory, Larry
Grimm, Mike
Groom, Darrell

Guenette, Jean
Guinn, Neal
Guthrie, Tony
Haggins, Don
Hakim, M. H.
Hale, Bruce
Hale, Mitch
Hall, Jeff
Hames, Michael
Hamilton, Cheryl
Hamilton, Kelly
Hamilton, Mark
Hammers, Jack
Handrahan, John
Hansen, Randall
Harder, Dave
Hardin, Jeffrey
Harding, Reginald
Hare, John
Harewood, Leslie
Hargrove, Donald, II
Harjo, Legus, Jr.
Harmon, Tim
Harper, David
Harper, Gary
Harrington, Doug R.
Harrington, Phillip
Harris, Jay
Harris, Kenneth
Harrison, David
Harrison, Michal
Hart, John
Hasler, Bobby
Hauenstein, Chuck
Hayes, David
Hayes, Michael
Haywood, Michael
Heaton, Geri
Helling, Scott
Helzer, Jeffrey
Henry, Tim
Hensley, Paul
Herd, Sam
Herndon, Grover
Herrera, Manuel
Herrmann, Joe
Herzog, Reid
Hester, Bert
Higdon, Gary
Highfill, Steve
Hill, Kerry
Hill, Lyle
Hill, Mike
Hinkle, Terry
Hintz, Paul
Hodges, Glenn
Hodges, Buddy, Jr.
Hofen, Jay Don
Hoffman, Roy
Hoisington, John
Hollingshead, Mark
Holt, Dale
Holt, Glenn
Holt, Ryan
Hoover, Greg
Hoover, Henry
Hoover, Jerry
Horath, Ronnie
Horn, Glen
Horn, Nicky
Horn, Trader
House, James
House, Katherine
Howard, Kenny
Howard, Tom
Hudler, David
Hudlow, Gary
Hudson, Gerald
Huffman, Geary
Hughes, Esperanza
Humphries, B. G.
Hunt, Dahlton

Hunter, Chris
Hunter, Michael
Hunter, Rickey
Hurst, Donna
Hutchison, James
Hyde, Travis D.
Ingram, Gerald
Inman, Angie
Isom, Mark
Jackson, Dan
Jackson, Danny
Jackson, Robert
Jacobs, Fowler
Jean, Kimberly
Jenkins, David
Jenkins, Eugene
Jobe, Sharon
Joe, Tom
Johns, Billy
Johnson, Belleva
Johnson, Butch
Johnson, Darran
Johnson, Gary
Johnson, Greg
Johnson, Joni
Johnson, Sheila
Johnston, Jon
Johnston, Raymon
Johnston, Roy, Jr.
Joiner, John
Jolly, Dan
Jones, Craig
Jones, Don
Jones, Eric
Jones, Gordon
Jones, Kelly
Jones, Larry
Jones, Mike
Jones, Mike
Just, Lyle, Jr.
Kannady, Sheldon
Kapke, Monty
Kappus, Eric S.
Kaufman, Joel, Jr.
Kays, David
Kear, Allen
Keenan, Kevin
Keith, Billy
Kemp, Carl
Kemp, Larry
Kennedy, Curtis
Kenney, Wesley
Kepford, Gary
Kerns, David
Kesler, Ronnie
Key, Michael
Keys, David
Kimberlin, P. D.
King, Greg
King, Richard
King, Steve
Kirk, Leroy, III
Kiser, Roger
Kline, Cindy
Klopfenstein, Ray
Knox, Terry
Koch, Randy
Kolp, Chuck, Jr.
Kosemund, Bradley
Kourtis, Karol
Kroutil, Cheryl
Kuebeck, Peter
Kugler, Tom
Kyle, Eddie
La Ferney, Kenny
Labude, Kevin
Lafferty, Burl
Lafoe, Mike
LaFollette, Gary
Lahr, Jerry
Lancaster, David
Lane, William

Larson, Jeffrey
Larson, Kenneth
Lassen, Thomas
Lassley, Gary
Ledbetter, Randel
Lee, David
Lee, Donnie
Lee, Finis
Lee, Norman
Legg, John
Lehman, Arthur
Lenington, Paul
Lentz, Steve
Leonard, Lisa
Lewelling, Carl
Lewis, Jeff
Lewis, Thomas, II
Ligon, John
Lingle, Timothy
Linkous, Eric
Lippard, Jon
Locke, James
Loeffelholz, Donald
Lohaus, Jason
Loman, Bradley
Long, Donna
Looney, Terry
Lopez, Benny
Loughmiller, Dan
Loughmiller, Tony
Loveless, Mark
Lowe, Dwight
Lowe, Kyle
Lucy, Roy
Lum, Ronald
Lumry, Mike
Lynch, Scott
Mabry, Terry
Mack, LaShon
Mack, Douglas
Madden, Michelle
Madrid, Bill
Mahen, Michael
Malicott, Jean
Mann, Cecil
Mantooth, Don
Marion, Vernon
Marlar, Cliff
Marlatt, Mark
Marshall, Justin
Marshall, Thomas
Martin, Don
Martin, Fredrick C.
Martin, Marcus
Martin, Mark
Martin, Tim
Mason, Eddie
Mason, Randy
Mateo, Robert
Mathews, Mike
Maxwell, Laureen
Mayo, Larry
McAfee, C. L.
McAlister, Shaun
McAnally, David
McAvoy, James
McBee, Matthew
McCandless, Ferrill
McCarty, Craig
McCarty, Wendell
McDaniel, Charlotte
McDonald, Ann
McFarland, Tom
McGehee, Jerrie
McKinney, Brian
McKinnis, Tom
McKinzie, Kenneth
McLaughlin, Pat
McMurtrey, Joe
McNutt, Larry
McRee, Harry
McVey, Ronald

Mead, Toby
Meadows, Linda
Melton, Kyle
Menchaca, Albert
Metzinger, Dale
Milam, Jane
Milanowski, Scott
Miller, Brent
Miller, Jim
Miller, Kay
Miller, Lajunta
Miller, Larry
Miller, Leonard
Miller, Paul
Miller, Ronnie
Millican, Steven
Minden, Louis
Minyard, Charles
Mitchell, Neil
Mize, David
Mobly, Mark
Monks, Leonard
Montgomery, Patty
Montgomery, Ted
Moon, Lisa
Mooney, Thomas
Moore, Howard
Moore, Robert
Morehead, Daniel
Morgan, Howard
Morgan, Mike
Morris, Danny
Morris, Harvey
Morris, Randy
Mount, Tina
Muck, Larry
Mullins, Greg
Murphy, Dean
Murray, Alvin
Murray, Mark
Myers, Steven
Nagy, Kevin
Nance, Robbie
Natt, Bruce
Neal, Beedy
Neal, Mitchell
Neil, Mark
Nelson, Allen
Nelson, Grady
Nelson, Phillipe
Newman, Michael
Newton, Delmer
Newton, Jimmy
Niccum, Wayne
Nichols, Robert
Nichols, Tommy
Nickel, Darrin
Niemyer, Chuck
Nightingale, M. D.
Nipper, Eric
Nobles, Thomas
Norman, Larry
Norton, Richard, Jr.
Nunnelee, D. Wayne
Nye, Pat
Odle, Donald
OKelley, Timothy
Oliver, David
Olmstead, Ted
Olsen, Dane
Olton, Derrick
Ortiz, Joseph
Oshel, Curtis
Overbay, Johnnie
Owen, Stephen
Owens, Don
Ozment, Tony
Page, Jim
Palmer, Larry
Palmore, Billy
Palmrose, Rick
Park, Mike

Parker, John
Parker, Nancy L.
Parks, Gary
Parks, Marcus
Parsons, Gary
Payne, Kenneth
Pearson, Bill
Perando, Doug
Percell, Gary
Perkins, Mel, Jr.
Perkins, Raymond, Jr.
Perry, Scott
Peters, Robert
Petree, Mike
Pfleider, Monty
Phillips, Mark
Pickle, Leroy
Pierce, Al
Pierce, Denny
Pierce, Donald
Pine, James
Pinkerton, Curtis
Pippin, Dale
Poe, John
Pool, Joseph
Porter, David
Posada, Andy
Potter, Larry
Potter, Mitch
Powell, Bryant
Powell, Howard
Power, Raymond
Prier, Jeff
Printup, Jon
Prough, Quay
Pryor, Betty
Puckett, Paul
Pyle, Cynthia
Rackley, Skip
Ragsdale, Joe
Rains, James
Rainwater, Derek
Rakosky, Jerry
Ramsey, Steve
Randle, Ted
Ranells, Billy
Raney, L. Farrell
Raof, Ebrahim
Ratliff, Montie
Rauser, Jim
Rawdon, Charles
Ray, Vindle
Reavis, Dennis
Reed, Curtis
Reese, D. Wayne
Reilley, Kirk
Reilly, David
Reyes, Richie
Reynolds, Tommy
Rhoten, Fred
Richey, Mark
Riess, Paul
Rigsby, Ray, Jr.
Robbins, Terry
Roberts, Doyle
Roberts, Lora
Robertson, Donald
Robertson, Joshua
Robertson, Larry
Robertson, Richard
Robinson, Teri
Robinson, Dan, Jr.
Rogers, Jarod
Rogers, Richard
Rogers, Steven
Root, Steven
Rose, Ginna
Rosenbaum, Paul
Ross, Toby
Rowe, Jimmy
Rowlett, Gary
Rubin, Mike

Ruiz, Carlos
Rushing, Richard
Rutter, John, III
Ruyle, Steve
Sallee, Raymond
Sanders, Gary
Sanders, Jay
Sanderson, Joseph
Satterfield, J. B.
Satterfield, Ron
Sauls, Leonard
Savage, Michael
Saxton, Pat
Scarberry, Buddy
Scarberry, Garland
Schat, Bobby
Schenberg, John
Schilling, Ron
Schmitz, William
Schroeder, Bob
Schultheis, George
Schultz, David
Scivally, Bobby
Scott, Clay
Scott, Gerald
Scott, Jerry
Scott, Louis
Self, Anthony
Self, Chad
Sever, Greg
Sewell, Danny
Shatto, Bobby
Shaw, Timothy
Sheffield, C. G.
Shephard, Larry
Sheppard, John
Shetley, Ryan
Sigler, Richard
Silverhorn, Warren
Simmons, Randall
Simon, Glenda
Sims, Bruce
Sinor, Ronnie
Sisco, J. R.
Sitton, Craig
Slayton, Gary
Slief, David
Smart, Ron
Smith, Brian
Smith, Dave
Smith, Gerald
Smith, Gregory
Smith, Karmon
Smith, Mike
Smith, Raymond
Smith, Sharon
Smith, Stanley
Smith, Steven
Smith, Stewart
Smith, Val
Smith, R. K., Jr.
Sneed, Larry
Snowden, Allen
Solenberg, John
Soutiere, Raymond
Sowle, Davin
Sparrow, Jim, Jr.
Spears, Billy, Jr.
Spess, Paul
Spicer, Sean
Splawn, Darryl
Stafford, Larry
Stambaugh, Gerry
Stamper, Donald
Stansberry, Randy
Staton, James
Steelmon, Wendell
Stephenson, Robert
Stepp, Michael
Stevens, Gary
Stevens, Ted
Stewart, Dennis

Stewart, Jim
Stickler, Phil
Still, David
Straka, Mark
Streater, David
Strickland, Thomas
Stripling, Jackie
Stubblefield, B. R.
Stukey, T. J.
Stutterheim, Monte
Swart, Coulter
Swift, Manuel
Sykes, Mitchell
Tackett, Jeff
Taite, Clarence
Talley, Jerry
Tatum, Bryan
Taylor, Kelly
Taylor, Mary
Teeples, Larry
Tennery, Michele
Terry, Sid, Jr.
Thomas, Gary
Thompson, D. C.
Thompson, Dallas
Thompson, Ellis
Thompson, Jim
Thompson, Rick
Thompson, Tim
Thornton, Michael
Thrash, Roy, Jr.
Thurman, Charles
Todd, Davie
Tooley, James
Tow, Wayne
Towery, Gale
Trammell, Linda
Trease, Randall
Trent, David
Trivitt, Donnie
Troxel, Vickie
Troyer, Dennis
Tuggle, Clifford
Tuley, Derrick
Turner, Cynthia
Turnipseed, Tammy
Ullom, Troy
VanBebber, Marvin
Vanfleet, Rod
Varner, Steve
Vasquez, George
Venter, Bob
Verser, Dan
Vest, Randall
Vinson, Richard
Vinson, Sharon
Voreis, Randy
Waddill, Connie
Walk, Roger
Walker, Jeffery
Walker, Robert
Walker, Vick
Walters, Jimmie
Ward, David
Ward, Jerry
Ward, Michael
Ward, Rickey
Warner, Jeff
Warren, Erv
Warren, Robert L., Jr.
Watkins, Larry
Watkins, Paul
Watkins, Steve
Watson, Gary
Watts, James
Webb, Chester
Webb, Mark
West, Robert
Westbrook, Leona
Weston, Virgil
Whalen, Mike
Whisenhunt, Glen

White, Austin
White, James
White, Jerry
Whitefield, Ronnie
Whitehead, Norman
Whitehouse, Steve
Whiten, O. Bryan
Whittaker, Ricky
Whitten, Jack
Wickware, Jason
Wiley, Mark
Wilhite, Kathleen
Williams, Bobby
Williams, Chuck
Williams, Kenneth
Williams, LaFayette, Jr.
Williams, Randal
Williams, Scott
Williams, Trey, III
Williamson, F. L.
Williamson, Robert
Wilson, Anna
Wilson, Jeff
Wilson, Nancy
Wilson, Nick
Wilson, Robyn
Wingo, Vollie
Winnard, Fred
Wiseley, Marissa
Witte, Tim
Wofford, Homer
Wolfe, Darrel
Wolfe, Robert
Woodard, Howard, Jr.
Woodring, Melvin
Woodruff, Howard, II
Woods, Robby
Woolever, Curtis
Woolverton, Jimmy
Workman, Russell
Workman, Jerry, Jr.
Worthy, Michael
Wright, James
Yost, Harvey
Young, Michael
Young, W. D.
Youngker, Randal

• POWER SUPPLY

Abney, Michael
Acedansky, Theresa
Adams, James
Adams, John
Adams, Judy
Adams, Robin
Aldridge, Jeffrey
Alfred, Steven
Allen, Paul
Allen, Norman, Jr.
Alley, Joe
Amos, Will
Anderson, Kenneth D.
Anson, Denise
Archer, Garry
Armstrong, Clayton
Arnold, James, III
Atchison, Samuel
Aust, Ed
Babb, Alan
Banks, Alan
Barkhimer, Carl
Barrett, W. L.
Beasley, Wayne
Belusko, John
Benham, Ford
Bevelhymer, Tony
Bevins, Bryan
Bigby, Karen
Birdsong, J. D.
Black, Douglas

Blansett, Steven
Blevins, Terry
Bohn, George, Jr.
Boles, Lisa
Bomgardner, Quentin
Bowden, John
Bowien, Billy
Brackett, Scott
Brady, Larry
Branecky, David
Brewster, Steven
Brien, Diana
Brimberry, J. Kenneth
Britt, Edgar
Brooks, Darryl
Brown, Larry
Brown, Robert
Brown, Ronald
Brown, Rufus
Brown, Tye
Bryant, James
Bunch, Terry
Burgess, Ricky
Burnett, Donald
Burns, Larry
Burns, Marlin
Butler, Daniel
Butler, Robert
Cain, Daniel
Callison, Tom
Calvert, Billy
Canada, John
Carroll, Robert
Carter, Bobby
Carter, David
Casey, Kelly
Cash, William
Castor, Cody
Cato, James
Cave, Jim
Chandler, Royce
Chriestenson, Leslie
Christensen, Jasper
Christie, Robert
Chung, Siew
Clark, Connie
Clary, Irby
Clayton, Dale
Clear, Gary
Clouse, George
Coburn, Floyd
Cochran, W. C.
Coffman, Jack
Conlee, Lonnie
Cook, Cheryl
Cook, Kendall
Cooper, Charles
Copus, J. L.
Cornish, Christopher
Corter, Thomas
Costello, John, Jr.
Couch, Thomas
Countess, Shane
Crabtree, C. W., Jr.
Craig, Michael
Crain, Timothy
Cranford, Robert
Cranford, Wayne
Cruse, B. G.
Curtis, Danny
Dailey, Randy
Darbison, Reginald
Davis, Benjamin
Davis, Cleveland, Jr.
Davison, Greg
Day, Jerry
Day, V. G.
DeArmond, Tony
Deaton, Tommy
Dillon, Mark
Dixon, Loyd
Dotson, J. C.

Doupe, Robert
Downey, H. R.
Downs, Ronald
Doyle, James
Driskel, Frankie
Drymon, James
Duck, Tim
Dunn, Patricia
Durossette, Jim
Duvall, Gary
Dyer, David
Eberle, Frank
Eberle, Raymond
Edgmon, David
Eller, Randy
Elliott, R. C.
Ellis, Randy
Emrich, Robert
Englebretson, David
Eno, Robert
Ensey, Robert
Epperson, Billy
Erwin, Stephanie
Evans, D. E.
Evans, Todd
Ewy, Dan
Faddis, Ken
Farguson, Bobby
Fassnacht, Michael
Felix, Eldon
Ferguson, Scott
Field, Steve
Fleck, Tammy
Fletcher, Gary
Flores, Noe
Ford, Robert
Ford, John, Jr.
Fortelney, Larry
Fortune, David
Foster, Bron
Foster, Charles
Foster, Eugene
Frazier, Earl
Freeman, Danny
Frisby, Don
Fry, Greg
Fullen, Doyle
Gabbert, Wade
Gaddy, Jody
Gaither, Thomas G., Sr.
Gallahar, Bailey
Gallaway, Edgar
Garner, Phillip
Gauntt, Timothy
Gent, Thomas
Gerdes, Bob
Gibbs, Michael
Gibson, Bill
Gibson, Randy
Gilbert, Randy
Gillispie, John
Gillogly, William
Gist, David
Gleason, Nickylee
Goebel, Summer
Gore, Matt
Gorman, Terry
Gould, Allen
Grace, Michael
Graham, Brian
Gray, Buddy
Green, Bill
Greenhagen, Travis
Grimes, Chris
Gritts, Shirley
Grover, Robert
Guinn, Jeff
Haken, Jana
Hall, Gilbert
Hall, Johnnie
Hall, Robert
Hall, D. W., Jr.

Hamilton, Dale
Hammack, Bret
Harden, Phil
Hare, Steven
Hargis, Lenny
Hargrove, Dennis R.
Harriet, Jon
Harris, Charles
Harris, Stephen
Harris, Timothy
Hatley, Larry
Hatley, Mark
Hatter, Bobby
Hauser, Robert
Hayer, Daniel
Haynes, Mark
Hedge, Andy
Heinken, Roger
Henderson, Leslie
Hendricks, Larry
Henson, Gary
Herriman, Jerry
Hightower, Oneal
Hise, Myron
Hoddy, Dennis
Hodges, Keith
Hoeltzel, Byron
Holloway, S. K.
Holmes, Larry
Hoover, Mack
Houston, Linda
Howard, Bobby
Howeth, James
Hubbard, Scott
Hughes, Norman
Hughes, William
Hull, Dale
Hunt, Ronald
Hunt, Ronny
Hunteman, Katie
Hurst, Michael
Hussong, Shawn
Hutchens, Terry
Hutchins, Edgar, Jr.
Hutson, Larry
Hyslope, Carl
Hyslope, Rick
Ingram, Curtis, Jr.
Irvin, Velma
Irving, Ronnie
Isom, Larry
Jackson, Michael
Jacobs, Ranie
Janssen, William
Jared, Jeff
Jennings, Richard
Johnson, Mickey
Johnson, Mike
Johnson, William
Johnston, Darrell
Jones, Boyd
Jones, Jerry
Jones, Quentin
Jones, Thad
Kain, Kevin
Kalicki, Louise
Kautzman, Brent
Keeley, Edward
Kendrick, Franklin
Kennedy, Billy
Keys, Johnnie
Kime, Jerry
Kinsey, Curtis
Kirk, Larry
Kirkendall, Danny
Kirkendall, J. R., Jr.
Kramer, Alan
Kuennen, Larry
Kymes, Don
Lane, Michael
Larrison, Glenn
Lashley, Kenny

Law, Billy, Jr.
Lay, Charles
Leach, Thomas
Lee, Hoy
Lee, Kevin
Lee, Randy
Leforce, Ronnie
Lempges, Donald
Lester, Bryan
Lewallen, Kerry
Lewis, Robert
Lewis, Robert
Lewis, Roberta
Lillard, William
Limke, Brian
Linton, Steve
Litzer, Richard
Loflin, Steve
Lone, Terry
Louthan, Jan
Low, Darrell
Lucy, Paul
Lyne, Douglas
Mackey, Jeff
Madron, Ronald
Mahan, Jesse
Maloy, Jackie
Manship, Alan
Manuel, Mark
Maples, Michael
Martin, Anthony
Martin, Jennifer
Martin, Larry
Martin, Melody
Martray, David
Mayberry, Edward
Mayle, Hershel
McAlister, Chris
McBroom, Shawn
McCain, Charles
McCarty, Mark
McClure, David
McCurry, Larry
McElroy, Debra
McGee, David
McGee, Roger
McGlothlin, Bob
McGreger, J. T.
McGuire, Mark
McLamore, William
McMahan, Sammie
McNeal, Alan
Medved, James
Meeks, Rodney
Megee, Tony A.
Mena, Tony
Menefee, Joe
Meyer, Jeff
Miller, Eldon
Miller, Randall
Miller, Terry
Miller, Wesley
Misenheimer, Jeff
Mitchell, Darlene
Mitchell, Jimmie
Moore, Allen
Moore, Ellis
Moore, Jimmie
Moore, Larry
Morland, Charles
Morphew, John
Morphis, Kim
Morris, Garry
Morse, Jimmy
Morse, Jody
Moses, Ralph
Mullen, Mark
Mullins, Philip
Mullon, Paul
Murray, Jimmy
Murray, Phillip
Myers, Harral, Jr.

Negelein, Walter
Newburn, Carl
Newton, Timothy
Nichols, Ricky
Nickel, Anthony
Norris, Kent
Nowakowski, Peter
Nunez, David
O'Brien, Thomas, Jr.
Oswalt, Walter
Oxley, Jason
Page, Johnnie, Jr.
Parham, John
Parker, D. L.
Parkinson, John
Parks, Larry
Parks, Steven
Patten, Charles
Payne, Marcus
Pepple, George
Perkins, Michael
Perry, Daniel
Perryman, Ann
Perryman, Jeremiah
Peyton, David
Phillips, Bob
Plagmann, Dean
Pogue, Danny
Points, Charlene
Pollard, Jerry
Pollock, Dean
Porter, Debra
Porter, James
Posey, Don
Postman, Mickey
Potter, Jerry
Presley, James
Presley, Terry
Prewett, Kelly
Pruitt, Jerry
Pryor, Calvin
Psomas, Clay
Puckett, Judy
Pyland, Victor
Qualls, Jim
Quary, Craig
Quiring, Patrick
Rambo, Barbara
Ratterree, Jimmy
Readdy, Saundra
Redden, Ronda
Reed, Derrick
Reich, Nickey
Relf, Donald
Reynolds, Michael
Richards, Joe
Richardson, Dale
Rieman, Chad
Rigney, Randy
Riley, Larry
Ringwall, Robert
Ritchie, Sheri
Robbins, Stanley
Roberson, Bobby
Roberts, Tommy E.
Robinson, William
Rodden, Rickey
Roddy, Mike
Roe, David
Romano, Mark
Rorex, Kenneth
Ross, Anthony
Ross, Charles
Rowland, Glenn
Royse, Raymond
Russ, Archie
Ryan, Tommy
Sanders, David
Sanders, Richard
Schmidlkofer, Frank
Schmunk, Annette
Schneider, Christopher

Schoenecke, Kelvin
Schultz, Steve
Schutte, John
Schutz, Frank
Scott, Kenneth
Scribner, Charles
Scroggins, Terry
Seelig, Steven
Seitz, Tommy
Sellers, Jerry
Seward, Johnny
Shannon, Scott
Sharp, Chris
Sharp, Robert
Shearhart, Bret
Sheik, Kelsey
Shelton, Stacy
Shiever, Linda
Shiever, Edward, Jr.
Shoemake, Roger
Sisk, Larry
Skarky, Susan
Smith, Bryan
Smith, Denice
Smith, Larry
Smith, Mark
Smith, Mark E.
Smithson, Chuck
Spears, Gerald
Spinks, Billy
Sprague, Richard
Standridge, John
Stanton, Keith
Staples, H. L., Jr.
Stearman, Jesse
Steele, Jeffrey
Stewart, David
Stidham, Scott
Stockton, Tammie
Stoup, Brandon
Straka, Carl
Stugelmeyer, Josh
Suppiah, Bahvahnie
Swearingen, Paul
Talamante, Orlando
Tapp, Larry
Tarver, David
Taybah, Alexander
Taylor, Jim
Thomas, B. M.
Thomas, Mark
Thomas, Max
Thompson, James
Thompson, Timothy
Thomson, David
Thrasher, Pete
Timmons, Ron
Todd, Wayland
Tolbert, Phillip
Torix, Louie
Trammell, Luther
Trammell, Steven
Tripp, Larry
Tubbs, Andy
Turner, Frederick, Jr.
Turney, Frank
Tyrrell, Kenneth
Vavra, Tom
Villines, Bob
Vinson, Donald
Vogle, Michael
Waggerman, Tony
Walker, Bobby
Walker, David
Waller, James
Walsh, Larry
Walters, Ronald
Ward, James
Warren, Josh
Warren, Justin
Warrior, Kenneth
Washington, King

Watt, Michael
Watters, Derrell
Waymire, Rick
Webb, Quinton
Weber, Michael
Wendling, John, Jr.
Whannel, Branden
Wheeler, David
White, Billy
White, Jeff
White, Richard
Whitmore, Robin
Wiedemann, Rodney
Wiggins, John, Jr.
Williams, Donald
Williams, Joseph
Williams, Larry
Wilson, Kenneth, Jr.
Wilson, Robert, Jr.
Witt, Timothy
Wood, Kenneth
Wood, Paul D.
Woods, Keith
Wright, Gary
Wright, Gary
Wright, Merl
Wyskup, Kathleen
Yott, Kenneth
Zachary, James
Zilem, Paul

• SHARED
SERVICES
Abernathy, Clayton
Adams, Dennis
Aldridge, Ron
Alexander, Kenneth
Anderson, Felisha
Armstrong, Jeff
Armstrong, Transic
Bain, William
Barnes, M. D.
Barton, Steven
Bates, Roger
Beaver, Terry
Bell, Christopher
Bernhardt, Jason
Bevers, Julia
Bielamowicz, Jerome
Blackburn, Gary
Blundell, Mark
Blundell, Mike
Boeckman, Dennis
Bohn, Lorna
Borjas, Benji
Bortz, Bob, Jr.
Brandt, Benjamin, Jr.
Brazille, Dewayne
Brodbeck, Katy
Brook, Michael
Broughton, Billy
Brown, Colin
Brown, David
Brown, Gary
Brown, Susan
Bryant, Mitchell
Buchanan, John
Canary, Karen
Canfield, Bill
Carr, David
Carrell, Jim
Caskey, Sherel
Chen, Yang
Chotkey, Sharon
Clark, Angela
Cockrell, Gary
Cole, Jeremiah
Cole, Tami
Converse, Ava
Cooper, Leamon
Cosby, Angela
Crall, Rosie

Criner, Thomas
Croslin, Larry
Cross, David
Cudjoe, Tagzmin
Cullen, Lindsay, II
Dagy, Bill, Jr.
Dallas, Linda
Daniels, Hubert
Davis, Alan
Davis, Paul
Davis, Paul, III
Davis, Steve
Deloney, Reginald
Dobry, Donald
Douglas, Michael
Dowdy, Floyd
Dowling, David
Dunkelgod, Dennis
Dunlap, Virginia
Egelston, Jeff
Ellis, Sophia
Ermey, Duane
Essex, Steve
Evans, Cindy
Faircloth, Jeffery
Farmer, Earl
Fennel, Jon
Ferrin, Mark
Fish, Michelle
Flanagan, Tommy
Flowers, John
Fowler, Joyce
Fowler, Leonard
Franklin, James, Jr.
Frazier, Darrell
Frederick, John
Gannon, Donnie
Garner, Susan
Gerdes, Steven
Givens, Elizabeth
Glasgow, Linda
Goetz, Dan
Gomez, Tony
Goss, Mark
Graves, Scott
Griffin, Ron
Grubbs, Michael
Grunsted, John
Guerrero, Izzy
Gunter, Gary, Jr.
Gurule, Mark
Guymer, Geoff
Halbig, Edward
Hamm, Mark
Harber, Larry
Harris, Randall
Harrison, Keith
Hart, Margaret
Harvey, Mark
Hatcher, Larry
Hendrickson, Tim
Hickman, Yvonne
High, Larry
Hines, Scott
Holbrook, Jay
Holbrook, Thelma
Holland, Paul
Hollis, David
Horner, Kathy
Howie, Janette
Hudson, J. D.
Hudson, Ray
Hulme, Judith
Hurt, John
Hyatt, William
Irwin, Bob
Irwin, James, Jr.
Ivey, Mark
Jakubs, Ronald
James, Kenneth
Jay, Daryl
Jefferson, Paul

Jennings, Steve
Jensen, Joy
Jett, David
Joern, Jerry
Johnson, Carl
Johnson, Johnny
Joiner, Fred
Jones, Brian
Jones, Christina
Jones, Willis
Jordan, Randy
Karn, Jim
Kataria, Hemant
Keahey, Sherry
Kelley, Ronnie
Kelly, Dennis
Kerr, Amy
Kerr, Pamela
Kitchens, Tracy
Knapp, Andy
Knight, D. G.
Kramer, Herb
Kunze, Jan
LaBrue, John
Lairamore, Carroll
Lang, Hannah
LaRue, Chris
Leyba, Lee
Lihyaoui, Kim
Linder, Joe
Lippoldt, William
Logan, Lisa
Lovelace, Mark
Lyons, Michael
Madden, Joel
Marler, David
Mayfield, Nancy
Maynard, Lance
McCampbell, James
McCarther, Urban
McClain, Glen
McClellon, C. G.
McCoy, Tina
McKnight, Craig
McNamee, Clyde, Jr.
Meadows, Stephen
Mercer, Don
Middlestead, Larry
Miller, Randy
Moffatt, Matt
Montgomery, Buck
Moore, Kemp
Moore, Kenneth
Morbley, Jim
Morgan, J. P.
Mosley, Wreyford
Motley, Stan
Muchmore, Carlos
Murphy, Jeremeh
Nair, Madhavi
Neisler, Joel
Nguyen, Lisa
Nichols, Cody
Nixon, Bruce
Nobert, Ivan
Nowakowski, Toby
O'Guinn, Melvin
Olson, Mike
Outon, Shirley
Overmeyer, Scott
Owen, Kendall
Padgett, Steve
Patterson, Jack
Patterson, Jeanne
Payne, Charles
Perry, Jesse
Perumalswamy, Raj
Peters, Ron
Peterson, Donald
Peterson, Tony
Petricek, Paul
Pfeil, Don

Phillips, Randolph
Phillips, Riley
Pitt, Kenneth
Pollock, Michael
Price, Billy
Prince, Gary
Pross, John
Pruitt, Raelene
Puckett, Stephen
Purintun, Darin
Raleigh, Jackie
Ramsey, Floyd
Randolph, Eric
Raymond, Kenneth
Reed, Larry
Retter, Don B.
Rhodes, Robert
Rice, James
Richard, Donald
Richardson, Richard
Ridlen, Kim
Roby, Russell
Rodden, Steven
Rohlmeier, Michael
Rosati, Sherry
Ross, Darryl
Ross, Todd
Rottmayer, Larry
Roy, David
Ryan, James
Sadler, Donna
Sampley, Nancy
Sanchez, Luis
Sanders, Andre
Sarcoxie, R. J.
Schnackel, Brian
Schuelein, Chet
Seems, Deena
Self, Laura
Sewell, Charles B.
Shook, Mark
Shutler, C. A.
Silmon, Turner, Jr.
Simpson, James
Smith, Stephen
Smith, Trei, III
Smoote, Oliver, Jr.
Spiva, Linda
Stewart, Jon
Stockton, Keith
Stone, Paula
Stone, Shirley
Storie, Curtis
Sullivan, Steve
Sumpter, Ron
Taylor, Richard
Taylor, Rick
Thomas, Jim
Thomas, Larry
Thomas, Paul
Thomason, Larry
Tilley, Kenneth
Tipton, Pamela
Towe, Jonathan
Tuggle, Laurie
Valdez, R. K.
Varughese, Sam
Vickers, L. D.
Walker, Jason
Ward, Shannon
Warrell, Laura
Watson, Lloyd
Webb, Dave
Weese, Mary
Weisenfels, Bill
Welch, Dedra
White, Margaret
Whitlock, Jack
Wickersham, Jerry
Wicks, George
Wilder, Stephanie
Williams, Zack

Wilson, James
Wilson, Rhevone
Wilson, Robert
Wilson, Steven
Winkler, David
Wolff, Jamie
Woodard, William
Wooden, Don
Workman, Stephanie
Yarholar, Doug
Yau, Zoe
Young, Kerri

APPENDIX II

OGE Energy Corp. Retirees as of January 1, 2002

Duplicate listings indicate two people with the same name.

Abbitt, V. E.
Abel, Jerry C.
Acord, Erick Z.
Adams, James C.
Adams, M. F.
Adkins, I. D.
Ahlert, Eugene J.
Ahmad, Nizam U.
Ainsworth, W.
Akin, Erwin
Akins, Bobby G.
Albers, J. L.
Alburtis, L. E.
Aldridge, Jerry E.
Alexander, Andy, Jr.
Alexander, Cleon C.
Alexander, Robert
Alexander, W. S.
Allen, Arman J.
Allen, Donald B.
Allen, James G.
Allen, M. H.
Allen, Patsy L.
Alley, George W.
Allyn, Eugene H.
Alvord, Thomas G.
Andersen, Loretta
Anderson, Billy D.
Anderson, Kenneth L.
Anderson, Lois M.
Anderson, R. G.
Anderson, W. A.
Anderson, Wallace R.
Andrews, Carl, Jr.
Andrews, Glen D.
Andrews, Johnny H.
Andrews, Margaret R.
Anglin, Benny C.
Antone, J. L.
Applegarth, R. W.
Appleyard, H. M.
Argo, James H.
Armarfio, James A.
Arms, Roger
Armstrong, Charley
Armstrong, T. L.
Arnett, Joyce C.
Ashley, Jimmy
Atkinson, Leroy
Atkinson, R. L.
Augustine, H. E.
Ausmus, Norma Jean
Austbo, Larry M.
Aynes, O. U.
Ayres, A. J.
Bacus, H. H., Jr.
Bahm, C. J.
Bailey, C. T.

Bailey, Phil
Baird, H. Wayne
Baker, Alton B.
Baker, M. R.
Baker, Mary C.
Baldwin, W. F.
Balkenbush, J. P.
Ball, Dee T.
Ballard, Donald R.
Baltes, Kenneth J.
Baltierra, Raul
Banard, Ira William
Banks, Richard C.
Bankston, Eddie L.
Barber, L. T.
Barber, Larry W.
Barclay, R. W.
Barker, Cleo A.
Barker, Thomas
Barkhimer, Steve
Barnes, Emily I.
Barnes, James
Barnes, Karey
Barnett, David
Barnett, Ethlyn J.
Barnett, Johnny E.
Barnicoat, R. E.
Barrett, F. L.
Barrick, H. D.
Barton, K. P.
Bateman, R. D.
Baucom, Tommy G.
Baxter, Billie J.
Baxter, James R.
Baxter, Wanda J.
Bays, Keith O.
Beach, R. B.
Beam, Grant
Beaman, E. I.
Beard, David R.
Beauchamp, Wynona H.
Beaver, Vernice L.
Beaverson, Paul R.
Beck, Charles W.
Beck, D. G.
Becker, James R.
Bellomy, Donna M.
Belshe, Thomas N., Jr.
Benford, Celma F.
Benge, D. P.
Bennett, Don P.
Bennett, Gleason D.
Bennett, Q. W.
Bennett, William R.
Bennyhoff, D. H.
Benton, Jerry L.
Benton, L. F.
Berryman, Billy M.
Best, Glenn D.
Best, Roy Clayton
Bevers, M. J.
Bibb, William L., Jr.
Biber, Mike
Bickford, C. W.
Biddie, K. W.
Biddle, K. D.
Biddy, J. E., Jr.
Biggs, Marion F.
Bigham, C. D.
Binkley, G. M.
Birchett, Dale
Black, A. L.
Blackburn, J. G., Jr.
Blackwell, J. A.
Blaine, Dianne L.
Blake, John R.
Blakely, W. H.
Blanchard, E. E.
Bland, George C.
Blaylock, F. L.
Blount, Jackie F.

Blue, L. A.
Boepple, L. R.
Bogart, John
Boggs, N. C.
Bolt, Lourene
Bond, Arthur, Jr.
Bonner, Billie E.
Booher, O. D.
Booker, D. H.
Boone, Virginia E.
Bortz, Marlene E.
Bottger, Ervin
Bowen, Eugene
Bowen, H. C.
Bowen, J. L.
Bowers, Phillip L.
Bowles, Zeb W.
Bowman, Loy
Boyd, H. L., Jr.
Boyd, Joann C.
Boyd, W. L.
Boyett, Lee J.
Brack, Fred
Bradley, Barbara J.
Bradley, Johnny R.
Bradley, Larry J.
Bradshaw, Corbet E.
Brady, R. L.
Bramlett, Travis M.
Brannum, James B.
Bray, Elzie R.
Bray, Afalo, Jr.
Bredel, Evelyn
Brehm, Norma Jean
Brewer, Boyne F.
Bridges, John W.
Bridgewater, Ronald C.
Briggs, James W.
Briggs, James W.
Brimm, Barbara A.
Brinkworth, T. H.
Britt, Buddy
Broaddus, Robert A.
Brooks, Avery L.
Brooks, G. W.
Brooks, J. C.
Brooks, J. R.
Brown, G. E.
Brown, Howard C.
Brown, Isaiah J.
Brown, Judy L.
Brown, Leon
Brown, Leroy
Brown, M. W.
Brown, Mary
Brown, Maxine
Brown, Ruby L.
Brown, Tommy N.
Brown, Warren
Browning, Judith
Broyles, Bobby L.
Bruce, Edwin M.
Bryen, Gordon L.
Buchanan, Charles L.
Buck, Homer T.
Buck, Robert L.
Buckmaster, James W.
Buettner, Kenneth J.
Bullard, Richard L.
Bunce, Bobby G.
Burch, Billy
Burch, Jim
Burch, K. E.
Burchette, S. L.
Burdick, John
Burdue, Donna M.
Burger, Earl
Burkhalter, M. E.
Burkhart, Harvey
Burleson, M. V.
Burlison, Bill Dean
Burmeier, J. C.

Burnsed, S. H.
Burr, William J.
Burrell, Samuel A.
Burris, L. A.
Burroughs, R. L.
Burton, D. A.
Bushorr, Ida V.
Butler, Charlie F.
Butler, Patricia A.
Butler, Raymond L.
Buxton, David
Byers, Edward
Bynum, Rex L.
Byrd, Paul D.
Byrnes, Wanda Sue
Cahill, L. E., Jr.
Cail, Bobby R.
Cain, Paul
Caldwell, Carl E.
Cale, D. L.
Callicoat, E. A. Z.
Calvert, Jerry L.
Campbell, Bill
Campbell, J. L.
Campbell, W. F.
Canada, Curtis O.
Candler, J. L.
Cannon, George E.
Cantrell, C. R., Jr.
Cantrell, D. M.
Capps, C. T.
Card, Wyman C.
Cardiff, Larry A.
Carlile, G. F.
Carman, George L.
Carpenter, George
Carpenter, Mike
Carter, J. W.
Carter, Jerry
Case, D. W.
Casey, J. D.
Casey, James W.
Casteel, M. L.
Cato, W. R.
Cavett, Mary J.
Chadwick, C. J.
Chaffin, E. D.
Chandler, Bobby S.
Chapman, G. W.
Chapple, Kenneth E.
Chenoweth, C. V.
Chesher, T. A.
Chester, Robert E.
Chicoraske, L. E.
Childers, James, Jr.
Childress, Thomas E.
Chitwood, Arthur L.
Christian, Linda M.
Christian, P. E.
Christner, Roy
Church, Billy
Church, Jerry L.
Cisper, Albert
Clark, Gwen
Clark, J. M.
Clark, Keith S.
Clarkson, Jimmy
Clift, C. E.
Cockriel, Beverly K.
Coffey, Bobbie D.
Coffey, Coy E.
Colbert, Harold C.
Cole, John P.
Cole, Rayburn
Coleman, William O.
Collier, A. G., Jr.
Collier, J. C.
Collins, B. R.
Collins, Frank
Colquitt, Glenn C.
Combes, Norman C.
Combes, Paul

Combs, George P.
Conger, Delbert D.
Conrad, John
Cook, Jimmy D.
Cook, Jimmy Ray
Cook, Karen L.
Cooley, D. W.
Cooner, Gary
Cooper, Dulcie G.
Cooper, Jack
Cooper, Jim
Cooper, Lawanna F.
Cooper, Marilyn C.
Cope, J. L.
Copeland, Charles C.
Corbin, Johnnie F.
Cordell, C. Rex
Corle, Frances
Cory, Ernest S.
Cosgrove, Leo C.
Cotton, G. W.
Coulter, D. B.
Council, G. C.
Cowden, C. L.
Cowherd, O. B.
Cowley, Josie M.
Cox, Arthur M.
Cox, J. W.
Cox, John W.
Cox, Lester D.
Cox, Marie A.
Cox, R. G.
Cox, Robert L.
Cox, W. E.
Crabb, Donna F.
Craft, Billy D.
Craig, B. R.
Cravatt, Norman E.
Creech, C. D.
Crockett, Bud
Cross, G. L.
Crowe, James E.
Crull, Raymond A.
Cullen, Lela A.
Cullers, Gerald W.
Cummings, James R.
Cummins, Barbara Jo
Curran, Mary F.
Curry, J. W.
Curry, Val H.
Cusick, J. E.
Dacus, Coy
Dale, Edwin Eugene
Dale, Jerry M.
Dale, Richard S.
Dalke, G. R.
Daniell, B. J.
Dansby, W. O.
Daubenspeck, A. O.
Daughtry, D. L.
Davee, John H., Jr.
Davis, Billy G.
Davis, Clifford R.
Davis, H. C.
Davis, J. D.
Davis, Jo Anne
Davis, Joe P.
Davis, Kenneth Paul
Davis, Kenneth W.
Davis, Marilyn
Davis, Marion
Davis, P. G.
Davis, Yvonne
Dawes, L. B.
Dawson, Elmer
Dawson, William B.
Dawson, Jack W., II
Day, Richard C.
Deaton, Walter
Deaton, William E.
Decamp, James A.
Deming, R. E.

Deskin, T. F.
Determan, J. L.
Devereaux, Merle E.
Dewbre, D. G.
Dicks, Manuel E.
Dilks, D. W.
Dillard, Harold W.
Dillard, Herman
Dillon, C. E.
Dixon, Lewis V.
Dobbs, J. W.
Dobbs, Richard L.
Dodd, Eugene A.
Dodd, Mark L.
Dodd, Ollen F.
Dodd, R. J.
Dodge, Bobby D.
Donham, S. M.
Dortch, Chuck
Doty, W. C.
Douglas, Cecil R.
Douglass, Benester
Dozier, Lawrence D.
Drew, E. S.
Droke, J. R.
Druiett, Gene A.
Dubois, N. A.
Duboise, W. W.
Dudley, Von Dale
Dunagan, George L.
Dunbar, F. E.
Duncan, Larry D.
Dunkins, Effie Jean
Durheim, Leroy W.
Dybendal, Garry A.
Dykes, B. E.
Earley, Charles D.
Earls, James R.
Earnest, Drennon
Ecker, George D.
Ecker, John
Eddy, Larry
Eden, J.
Edwards, J. O., Jr.
Edwards, Pete
Eeds, Carroll R.
Eggers, Ronald W.
Eisenhour, H. L.
Elam, Ray L.
Elmore, Charles B.
Elmore, S. L.
Emerson, Victor
Emmons, Jerry D.
Engel, Mary
England, Jimmy Ray
Englebretson, D. L.
Ennis, Bill G.
Epperson, John
Ervin, H. H.
Erwin, T. C.
Estes, B. M.
Evans, B. R.
Evans, Noce
Evans, O. M.
Evans, Ralph J.
Ewell, C. L.
Ezell, R. H.
Factor, Tommy
Faires, R.
Faith, D. C.
Faler, B. J.
Fallen, Norman
Farber, C. G.
Farley, E. E.
Farley, J. Mark
Farmer, J. L.
Farquhar, Jimmy R.
Farris, Jack L.
Fehring, Dorothy J.
Felix, David L.
Felkins, Odis D.
Fender, Charles M.

Fent, Linda K.
Fergason, Howard D.
Ferguson, Bernard A.
Ferguson, Billy D.
Ferguson, Gerald D.
Ferling, E. L.
Feuerborn, C. E.
Fiegel, Euleta M.
Fielder, Mark
Fields, Kenneth I.
Finch, W. E.
Fincher, Myrna D.
Findley, B. C.
Fischer, Charles W.
Flanagan, G. W.
Flanary, Joe
Fleener, B. R.
Fleming, Anna Mae
Fleming, Oran R., Jr.
Floyd, Charles M., Jr.
Floyd, Winston
Flynn, M. E.
Flynn, W. P.
Fogle, John
Foley, David B.
Fondren, Don P.
Foraker, Morris E.
Forbes, E. E.
Ford, Elgie C.
Fore, J. T.
Forrest, Kenneth W.
Foster, Bryan T.
Foster, Charles
Foster, Frank T.
Fountain, J. E.
Fowler, Don M.
Fowler, Truman, Jr.
Fowler, W. D.
Fox, Marsha
Francen, Donald G.
Frazier, Kenneth F.
Freed, John D.
Freeman Lewis, B.
   Jonelle
Freeman, Claybourn
Freeman, Guy C.
Freeman, Ronald G.
Fry, Boyd D.
Fry, Carol Sue
Fulks, Adis P.
Fullenwider, N. L.
Fuller, Norman
Fuller, W. C., Jr.
Gaede, Glenn R.
Galbreath, Lola F.
Gambel, Earnest E.
Gann, Billy G.
Gann, Richard
Gard, Ralph
Gardner, Don B.
Gardner, Donald L.
Gardner, Gary
Gardner, Judith G.
Gardner, Mac A.
Gardom, F.
Garner, Boyd W.
Garner, Jerry
Garvin, Jimmy C.
Gathright, Jack W.
Gattenby, F. W.
Gaylor, T. L.
Geissler, Leroy W.
George, R. D.
George, Thomas H., Jr.
Ghassemi, Linda
Gibbons, G. L.
Gibbs, Dan M.
Gibson, Tom E.
Gilbert, Ozell
Gillham, M. P.
Gilliam, Claudine
Gilliam, James T.

Gilroy, Billie J.
Gilson, Jerry O.
Gist, James E.
Glenn, W. H.
Goad, Clarence E.
Godfrey, L. R.
Goforth, Murray G.
Golden, Haskell L.
Goldsmith, R. O.
Goodale, Jerry E.
Goodman, J. K.
Goodman, J. L.
Goodpasture, D. L.
Goodson, Gail N.
Goosman, C. E.
Goosman, David M.
Gordon, D. D.
Gordon, Dan
Gothard, Jimmie A.
Gothard, Linda
Gould, Bobby J.
Govett, Jerry L.
Gow, R. B.
Gragert, Merton W.
Graham, D. M.
Graham, Harold, Jr.
Gramlich, Ruby J.
Grandstaff, Ray
Granger, Robert W.
Grant, Nina
Graves, Earl H.
Graves, Jimmie L.
Gray, L. A.
Grayson, Eugene
Green, Herman V.
Green, Lloyd E.
Green, Maurice C.
Green, R. P., Jr.
Greenlee, O. G.
Greer, G. E.
Griffin, T. L.
Grimes, E. R., Jr.
Griner, Kirby D.
Groesbeck, J. V.
Gross, Phillip E.
Grover, H. Leon
Grow, J. N.
Guerra, Julian C.
Gum, Russell D.
Gunnell, Glynna M.
Guthery, Anna
Hacker, D. V.
Hacker, R. R.
Haddican, Robert L.
Hahn, H. A.
Haley, Artie J.
Hamilton, R. P.
Hamman, Jim
Hammond, W. C.
Hammons, E.
Hamon, Floyd L.
Hampton, James D.
Hanes, Harold
Hanneman, Joe A.
Hanson, Sigurd
Hanus, Max Conrad
Harader, F. L.
Harber, L. J.
Harbour, J. W., Jr.
Hardcastle, F. D.
Harden, Delbert A.
Hardnett, John D.
Hardy, Reginald D.
Hargraves, Elston
Hargrove, John J.
Harjo, A. L.
Harkey, G. P.
Harlan, Ross E.
Harmon, G. L.
Harper, Chester Lee
Harper, Earl G.
Harper, Harlis E.

Harraman, Bertha A.
Harrell, C. E.
Harris, Fay Dee
Harris, Harvey R.
Harris, James B.
Harris, James M.
Harrison, Charlotte
   Gail
Harrison, J. D.
Harrison, Jimm L.
Harrison, William P.
Harwell, Peggy J.
Hathaway, Billy L.
Hawkins, Carol A.
Hawkins, James A.
Haws, Hubert, Jr.
Hay, D. H.
Haydon, Willard
Hayes, Robert L.
Haygood, Lloyd
Hays, Edmund D.
Hazley, Cecil L.
Head, H. L.
Hearn, William L.
Heinen, James T.
Heiss, Herbert H.
Helms, Harvey J.
Helms, R. W.
Hembree, Otis Lee
Hembree, Jess E., Jr.
Hemken, Imogene
Henderson, E. L.
Henderson, Jean H.
Henke, Carl R.
Henke, E. H., Jr.
Henley, B. G.
Henneke, C. O.
Henry, Ron H.
Henry, Ronald
Henry, Virginia A.
Henslee, E. E., Jr.
Hensley, Morris
Herbert, G. L.
Herndon, William R.
Herth, Marty
Hess, William E.
Hewitt, Ronald
Heydman, B. T.
Hibbert, M. A.
Hickerson, C. J.
Hickey, J. C., Jr.
Hicks, Dale
Hiett, M. F.
Higbie, R. Dardis
Hilger, James A.
Hill, A. D.
Hill, H. L.
Hill, William F.
Hines, John L.
Hines, V. M.
Hirst, J. W.
Hiseley, James L.
Hitt, Marvin D.
Hitt, Stanley J.
Hobson, Bobby R.
Hodgden, William M.
Hodges, James D.
Hoefar, Gary D.
Hoehner, Kathryn
Hoffman, William C.
Hoke, T. R.
Hoklotubbe, Linda
Holasek, V. James
Holcomb, Mildred T.
Holder, Thomas P.
Holland, John A., Jr.
Holland, Katie
Holland, R. W.
Holley, H. C.
Holly, Ted D.
Holmes, Bessie M.
Holsapple, Frank C.

Holt, D. J.
Holt, Howard
Hood, Elmer E.
Hood, R. C.
Hood, R. D.
Hood, W. A.
Hope, Louis
Hopfer, Glen D.
Hopkins, Charles W.
Hopkins, F. B.
Horst, David L.
Horton, H. B.
Hosier, E. E.
Hostetler, Magenta L.
Hostler, J. F.
House, Douglas R.
Householder, C. D.
Houston, Edgar
Howard, A. Dwain
Howe, D. G.
Howell, A. S., Jr.
Howell, C. F.
Howell, E. Ray
Hubbard, H. C.
Hubl, David
Huckleberry, V. T.
Hudgins, D. L.
Huff, Wallace
Huggins, Jimmy L.
Hughes, Richard W.
Hulbert, David E.
Hull, L. D.
Hurst, Harvey G.
Hurst, Juanita Patton
Husband, W. H.
Hutchcraft, Norma J.
Hutson, James C.
Hutton, E. J.
Ihle, Slonia M.
Iker, Archie R., Sr.
Iliff, R. D.
Ille, Terry M.
Ingraham, Pamela S.
Ingram, H. B.
Ingrum, L. F.
Intemann, Wayne L.
Irons, F. R.
Irons, Raymond W.
Irvin, Anderson
Irwin, Haskell W.
Isaac, Linda J.
Isaacs, Gary
Isaacs, Ronald
Jacks, Glendon
Jackson, J. H.
Jackson, N. K.
Jacobs, James D.
James, Grant
James, Shelton
Jantz, Roger L.
Janzen, P. R.
Jared, J. S.
Jaronek, R. F.
Jaynes, Floyd W.
Jenkins, Barbara
Jenkins, Glen E.
Jenkins, Joe
Jenson, Euel T.
Jernigan, K. R.
Jestes, Betty J.
Jestice, Billy J.
Johnson, Charles
Johnson, Donald M.
Johnson, E. C.
Johnson, E. R.
Johnson, Frank S.
Johnson, I. L.
Johnson, Inez
Johnson, James Lee
Johnson, James R.
Johnson, Lonnie
Johnson, Riley E.

Johnson, Robert E.
Johnson, Thomas E.
Johnson, William C.
Johnson, William D.
Jones, Bettie Jo
Jones, Billy B.
Jones, Bob D.
Jones, Chester L.
Jones, Darrell J.
Jones, Earl W.
Jones, Glenn G.
Jones, J. F.
Jones, Jack Darwin
Jones, Joyce M.
Jones, K. W.
Jones, Lewis W.
Jones, Lynn A.
Jones, Marlin D.
Jones, O. Earl
Joray, C. R.
Jordan, Eugene C.
Jurey, Dwight
Kaiser, Edward F.
Keck, Joe A.
Keck, Roy W.
Keech, Kenneth
Kelley, Grady Steve
Kelley, J. Paul
Kelley, Joel C.
Kelley, Patricia
Kelly, Howard Al
Kelly, Donald E.
Kemp, Ola Mae
Kennedy, B. L.
Kepler, Dorothy G.
Kerce, J. K., Jr.
Kerr, Herb T.
Ketcher, Ray C.
Ketchersid, K. A.
Kilmer, Lauren E.
Kincaid, W. R., Jr.
King, Harley Ted
Kinnamon, T. H.
Kinnear, Kenneth
Kinslow, Sue
Kirk, Ardyce A.
Kirk, Lawrence L.
Kirk, William B.
Kisor, T. E.
Kizziar, Gene
Klaus, Bob W.
Klein, Gary B.
Klepper, Dortha H.
Knowles, Winfred R.
Knox, K. G.
Knupp, Gary
Koch, Jack
Koehl, James B.
Koehn, Jim D.
Krause, H. F.
Krieg, R. W.
Krohmer, M. F.
Kuper, M. J.
Kusler, Franklin D.
Lahue, L. L.
Lair, W. L.
Lamb, E. R.
Lance, Sharon K.
Landers, John A.
Landes, Dan D.
Lane, Sally K.
Lang, Albert A.
Langdon, Ronald R.
Langer, L. A.
Langston, E. W.
Lanier, Floyce
Lanier, Gerald C.
Lanier, Larry A.
Lantz, Carol
Lantz, M. E.
Larue, K. R.
Lasanta, Mildred

Lasarsky, Stanley G.
Lasiter, James P., Jr.
Lau, D. M.
Lawrence, Andrew L.
Lawrence, Elton L.
Lawrence, Geneva P.
Laws, L. H.
Laws, Richard D.
Lawson, L. D.
Layman, Wayne W.
Leake, Cloyce V.
Leavitt, Richard E.
Lee, Gertrude E.
Lee, Mitchell
Lee, Sylvia A.
Lemaster, J. W.
Lemons, Kenneth L.
Lemons, Lavonia O.
Lenhart, Norman J.
Lesch, Henry F., Jr.
Leslie, Edwin M.
Lester, Alice Kay
Lewis, B. J.
Lewis, Billy Wade
Lewis, Curtis L.
Lewis, J. B.
Lewis, Jackie E.
Liles, B. W.
Liljestrand, J. E.
Lindsey, David
Lindsey, Emma J.
Lindsey, Pat N.
Lingo, Gordon
Linn, Rees G.
Linville, Robert E.
Little, G. A.
Little, John E.
Littleton, Tom
Liverson, Thomas E.
Lloyd, Arnold D.
Lloyd, Bobby Lee
Lloyd, W. D.
Lock, Orvel
Lodes, George M.
Loggins, Mayeola
Long, George W.
Long, Roy K.
Lopp, Walter E., Jr.
Lorenz, Donald E.
Lounge, Whitney
Louthan, M. G.
Love, D. R.
Love, John F., Jr.
Love, Joyce
Low, J. C.
Lowe, Jerry D.
Lowry, Jon W.
Loyall, M. R.
Lucas, Tom W.
Luckhart, William E.
Luis, Harold E.
Lynch, Edward
Lynch, Harry J.
Lynn, E. V.
Lyons, A. L.
Lyons, Jim L.
Mabe, Arr Cee
Mabry, E. J.
Macarty, F. M.
Mackey, R. F.
Maddux, James W.
Mahan, Eugene
Main, B. L.
Major, W. A.
Mangold, Richard L.
Manis, Elda A.
Manning, John L.
Manuel, J. J.
Marchant, Bobby J.
Marcott, J. E.
Maris, R. H.
Marris, Wood

Martin, Barbara J.
Martin, Bob D.
Martin, Donald C.
Martin, E. L.
Martin, H. J.
Martin, T. L.
Martin, V. R.
Martin, W. B., Jr.
Martindale, W. G.
Mashburn, W. N.
Matlock, H. L.
Matlock, Troy W.
Maxwell, C. E.
Mayes, Sharon M.
Mays, Kenneth R.
McAlister, William O.
McBride, Betty L.
McBride, Dorothy J.
McBurnett, Robert L.
McClellon, J. H.
McClendon, Earl O., Jr.
McClure, Buddy G.
McClure, D. A.
McClure, Patsy R.
McComber, Lester W.
McCormick, George L.
McCoy, Cecil
McCoy, Donald E.
McCracken, R. C.
McCraw, M. K.
McCurry, Jerry
McDaniel, M. L.
McDonald, Regina J.
McDonald, T. W.
McDowell, J. W.
McDowell, R. L.
McElroy, L. L.
McElroy, Russell T.
McFarlane, G. A.
McFerrin, Walter R.
McGaha, O. D.
McGahey, Judy
McGee, Dee
McGinnis, Jimmie L.
McGoodwin, B. P.
McGrew, Donnie R.
McGuire, Mary D.
McGuire, Max L.
McIntosh, George
Mckeown, Jack
McKey, Marion L.
McMahan, Jimmie L.
McMillan, Harold E.
McMillin, John P.
McMullen, Ernest L.
McNac, Wardell
McNally, Alleyene B.
Mead, Thomas N.
Medlock, Billy J.
Meeh, David W.
Mefferd, Charles
Meier, R. C.
Menie, Jack R.
Menifee, Floyd J.
Meredith, G. A.
Merrick, K. L.
Messner, Betty Jean
Middleton, C. W.
Miller, Carolyn L.
Miller, Dyrl
Miller, F. M., Jr,
Miller, Frank A., Sr.
Miller, H. G.
Miller, Jay
Miller, Joe M.
Miller, L. J.
Miller, W. T.
Miller, William C.
Mills, Pershing F.
Millsap, Harold J.
Minshall, H. E.
Mitchell, Charles K.

Mitchell, Dale L.
Mitchell, Mary
Mitchell, Michael V.
Moffat, I. E.
Moler, William J.
Moon, James C.
Mooney, Joseph J.
Mooney, Larry L.
Moore, D. C.
Moore, Edwin B., Jr.
Moore, James W.
Moore, Jimmy C.
Moore, Roger A.
Moore, Thomas C.
Moore, Tom
Moore, W. D.
Moore, William C.
Morgan, Billy Bob
Morgan, Floyd R.
Morgan, Gerald F.
Morgan, Jack D.
Morgan, James H.
Morgan, Vernon E.
Morris, B. C.
Morris, F. F., Jr.
Morris, Patricia E.
Morrison, C. R.
Morse, Eddie
Morton, E. M.
Moseley, Buddy R.
Mount, Sondra Jean
Mulkey, Lila N.
Mull, A. R.
Mullen, C. M.
Mullin, J. R.
Mullins, L. C.
Mullins, Robert L.
Mullins, Tim
Murdoch, Thomas F.
Murphey, Kenneth L.
Murphy, F. G.
Murphy, Harriet B.
Murphy, Ocus W.
Murray, Richard D.
Murrell, Martha H.
Muzny, C. V.
Myers, Joseph B.
Myers, L. C.
Myers, Robert L.
Nabors, Bill F.
Narry, Michael
Nash, Mack I.
Nation, Doris
Navarre, Roberta L.
Neal, Jesse G.
Nelson, Harry E.
Netherton, Truman H.
Neugebauer, Tommy L.
Newberry, Imogene
Newell, Larry
Newman, G. E.
Nichols, James H.
Nichols, Jerry L.
Nichols, Paul
Nicholson, John
Nickel, Melvin D.
Niles, L. E.
Nix, Richard
Nixon, Truman L.
Noakes, D. R.
Nolin, J. D. K.
Norlin, E. D.
Norman, Terry H.
Norton, Thurman
Norton, Velma J.
Norvell, Sam H., Jr.
Nowlin, Mary J.
Nunn, Robert W.
Nutter, Jimmie C.
Oberlender, Joann
Obrien, R. J.
O'Conner, Richard

Odell, J. C.
Odell, Johnny A., Jr.
Oelke, Paul G.
Ogg, J. R.
Oliver, T. F.
Oneal, Billy A.
Oneal, Billy G.
O'Neal, Brenton M.
O'Neal, James R.
O'Neil, Marvin D.
Oreilly, Minnie I.
Orr, K. C.
Orr, Norman
Osage, Rita M.
Osborn, Jerry
Osborn, Mary K.
Osborne, Julian E.
Otis, E. L.
Ott, Kenny
Owen, Joseph J.
Owen, Perry D.
Owens, Billy J.
Page, J. A.
Page, James R.
Page, Kenneth D.
Palmer, Carmelita C.
Palmer, K. R.
Palmer, Lloyd L.
Parish, Rufus L.
Parker, Jim D.
Parker, Russell D.
Parkins, Hubert M.
Parmeter, Don F.
Parsons, H. G.
Patterson, Claudy L.
Patton, Charles E.
Patton, W. L.
Paul, Herman J.
Payne, McMillan
Payne, Patrick Kent
Payne, T. J.
Payne, William E.
Peavler, Amos C.
Peavler, James M.
Peer, David
Pemberton, J. M.
Pembrook, Harley
Pennington, Cecelia J.
Pennington, Robert R.
Perfect, Leon Will
Perry, Fred T., II
Persons, R., Jr.
Peterman, Joe R.
Peters, J. L.
Peters, Lloyd
Peters, Martin C.
Peters, V. D.
Petricek, B. J.
Pettyjohn, Cathryn
Pfrimmer, R. W.
Phillips, Murray R.
Pickens, Glennon B.
Pickering, R. L.
Pierce, Charles R.
Pierce, V. G.
Pippin, A. L.
Pippin, Clarence H.
Pirtle, J. E.
Pittman, Joe
Pitts, J. R.
Plyler, Linda M.
Poe, Herbert L.
Poe, Richard R.
Poindexter, H. D.
Pollock, Ted F.
Pool, O. F.
Porter, Clinton
Porter, James M.
Ports, Richard
Poulter, Karen K.
Powell, Charles F.
Powell, James W.

Powell, Pamela
Poyner, J. E.
Pratt, Virgil L.
Preno, R. M.
Prewitt, Connie
Pribble, E. W., Jr.
Price, Garland W.
Price, Kenneth
Price, Stewart
Prigmore, L. E.
Pritchard, P. W.
Prock, Jerry L.
Pruitt, Douglas L.
Pruitt, John C.
Pryor, Edward
Puckett, E. Raye
Pumphrey, Carolyn R.
Purvis, B. D.
Puryear, Linda A.
Qualls, Jack W.
Quincy, William W., Jr.
Raba, Roger L.
Rader, Bob
Ragland, Jimmy V.
Ragsdale, Thomas
Ramsey, Elvie D.
Ramsey, Mike
Ramsey, R. D.
Ramsey, Thelma R.
Raper, Russell
Rasberry, Helen P.
Ray, Carl E.
Ray, H. E.
Rayburn, G. L.
Rayon, Cecil R.
Reading, Kenneth
Real, Starr
Reather, Robert J.
Recknagel, Jaclyn L.
Rector, J. E.
Reece, Ivy, Jr.
Reece, Kenneth V.
Reece, Leroy
Reed, Earl S., Jr.
Reed, Ronnie M.
Reeder, Marjorie L.
Reese, Neal F.
Reese, Ruth I.
Reeves, Roy A.
Regier, D. G.
Reynolds, Joe C.
Reynolds, Mayrene
Rhodes, David
Rhodes, Virginia L.
Richert, R. L.
Riddle, Amy A.
Riddle, Ted L.
Riggs, James W.
Riley, E. L.
Ritchie, H. L.
Rivers, William L.
Rives, James D.
Roberts, C. D.
Roberts, Carl E.
Roberts, Nancy J.
Robertson, C. E.
Robinson, J. A.
Robinson, Mozelle
Robinson, R. S.
Robinson, Reed Wayne
Robinson, Stella I.
Robison, J. W.
Rockett, Marianna
Rockman, M. W., Jr.
Roe, Don
Rogers, C. L.
Rogers, H. R.
Rogers, James H.
Rogers, Joy
Rogers, Laurence B.
Rogers, Ralph E.
Rogers, William L.

Romine, John
Rooks, E. A., Jr.
Rorex, Caryle A.
Rose, James D.
Rose, Michael
Ross, Danny
Roth, Ronald R.
Rouse, Jean M.
Rowland, F. H.
Ruby, Bruce C.
Rudd, Marylyn J.
Ruhl, K. F.
Rushing, Dale
Russell, J. D.
Russell, Jess L.
Russell, Lee E.
Russell, R. W.
Ruth, Kenneth E.
Rutherford, E. R.
Rutherford, H. F.
Rutherford, J. I.
Rutledge, Charles O.
Rutter, E. J.
Ryal, Janice
Ryan, Patrick J.
Sadler, A. L.
Sallee, George T.
Sanders, B. R.
Sanders, David C.
Sanders, Freda C.
Sanders, Thomas D.
Sanders, R. D., Sr.
Sanderson, Lloyd R.
Sartain, R. R.
Satterfield, F. D.
Saulsberry, R. J.
Savage, Wanda Ruth
Sawyer, Gene D.
Schagunn, James O.
Scheffe, Kenneth R.
Scheier, Joseph
Schell, Gale A.
Schier, Paul W.
Schimmel, Cherlyn K.
Schindler, Nora M.
Schmidt, Edward
Schneberger, L. D.
Schoonover, C. E.
Schoonover, Elvin F.
Schrodt, Lois
Schwab, Lester W.
Schwarz, G. F.
Scott, Alvin N.
Scott, Cliff
Scott, Harold E.
Scott, Roma D.
Scott, Roy J.
Scroggin, G. G.
Scroggins, Junior L.
Segler, Mary
Self, Howard
Sellers, P. L.
Sellman, R. A.
Sexton, H. A.
Shahan, R. Thomas
Shankster, J. L.
Shaunty, Dorotha M.
Shaw, Robert D.
Shaw, W. T.
Sheckels, J. L.
Shed, Roberta I.
Sheehy, Raymond D.
Sheets, Jack D.
Sheline, Paul R.
Shelton, Cecil E.
Shepherd, K. D.
Sheppard, J. W.
Shilling, James
Shirley, C. A.
Shobert, E. R.
Shook, Billy B.
Short, John R., Jr.

Shrier, J. L.
Shriver, J. F.
Shropshire, Gale A.
Shults, B. G.
Shutt, Earl L.
Siler, Mike D.
Siler, Troyce C.
Simmons, Edward F.
Simmons, Esther
Simon, C. C., Jr.
Simpson, Burton A.
Simpson, John W.
Sinclair, A. L.
Singer, Rod
Singleton, J. R.
Singleton, John
Sisney, Shirley B.
Sites, Paul W.
Sites, W. E.
Sizemore, Woodrow W.
Skaggs, Cecil D.
Slief, Laurence O.
Sloan, Franklin P.
Sloan, Sharon S.
Smiley, Mike
Smith, Arthur L.
Smith, B. L.
Smith, Cleveland C.
Smith, Donald W.
Smith, Elwood E.
Smith, Gary D.
Smith, Harold E.
Smith, Harold L.
Smith, Jack E.
Smith, Jackie W.
Smith, Jerry D.
Smith, John T., Jr.
Smith, Joyce J.
Smith, K. R.
Smith, Kenneth L.
Smith, M. B.
Smith, Myron
Smith, R. E.
Smith, Ralph L.
Smith, Robert H.
Smith, Roy G.
Smith, S. C.
Smith, Stanley A.
Smith, Ted W.
Smithee, Homer L.
Smithee, Ronny T.
Smithson, Etta L.
Sneed, John E.
Snow, Harvey R.
Snow, L. D.
Snow, Nancy L.
Soles, Robert
Solomon, L. O.
Sommer, W. E.
Sparks, R. E., Jr.
Speak, Edna C.
Spears, Charles A.
Spears, Richard L.
Speer, D. A., Jr.
Spencer, J. J.
Spiers, F. R.
Spillers, R. T.
Springer, G. W.
Spurrier, J. A.
Srum, Robert
Stahlheber, W. L.
Staley, D. E.
Standridge, Renona R.
Stangle, B. J.
Stanley, Sharon
Stark, W. L.
Starnes, John T.
Stead, V. L.
Stedman, Dennis L.
Stephens, Donna
Stephens, George
Stephens, M. H.

Sterling, J. D.
Stevens, Gale L.
Stevens, J. E.
Stevens, Larry G.
Stevens, Ronald P.
Stevenson, Janice
Stewart, Barbara A.
Stewart, Floyd W.
Stewart, Fred, Jr.
Stiles, Jimmie D.
Stilwell, Marshia
Stoll, Dale A.
Stoll, John
Stone, F. H.
Stone, Fred C.
Stone, R. T.
Stoner, Kenneth R.
Stout, Robert L.
Stratton, Charles L.
Stretch, John D., Sr.
Stroope, Herman D.
Stroup, C. B.
Strunk, Donnie
Sturdevant, W. A.
Sullins, Richard
Sullivan, Marvin L.
Sullivan, Warren G.
Sutton, R. L.
Swafford, A. D.
Swafford, Vernon Y.
Swarb, Luther Eston
Sweet, Elvin W.
Syrles, R. L.
Tabor, Jim L.
Talkington, Ronald J.
Talley, Jack
Talley, W. N., Jr.
Talton, Gay
Taylor, B. L.
Taylor, Charles L.
Taylor, Howard T.
Taylor, Willie
Taylor, Yula T.
Tennell, R. E.
Tenpenny, Leroy
Thies, Arlene
Thomas, J. C.
Thomas, Linda
Thompson, C. P.
Thompson, Dwaine
Thompson, Jerry
Thompson, John T.
Thompson, Siegrid
Thornton, H. E.
Thorpe, Miriam R.
Threadgill, Imogene
Tiemann, L. D.
Tifft, Jerry Ray
Tilly, Vernon
Timmons, Donald F.
Tingle, Wanda Joy
Tipton, Keith
Toews, Ruben
Tompkins, W. D.
Toran, William H.
Towers, Myron D.
Towle, James P.
Trent, F. J.
Trent, James A.
Troyer, Danny J.
Trumbly, Barbara J.
Tucker-Newton,
   Penolia M.
Tuley, Cliff
Tuley, T.
Tully, B. G.
Turner, Chester L.
Turner, Fred
Turner, R. D.
Tyler, Richard L.
Tyler, Ted
Tyo, Samuel E., Jr.

Tyree, Charles L.
Uffen, Kenneth P.
Underwood, Homer M.
Unruh, Loel D.
Upchurch, Cleva
Uselton, Vester L.
Vann, Billie J.
Vanscyoc, F. A., Jr.
Vaughn, D. E.
Vaughn, H. B.
Veal, C. C.
Vice, Carolyn K.
Vincent, Tom
Vinson, John M.
Vinyard, N. L.
Voss, Doris L.
Voyles, Clyde, Jr.
Waddle, Herley W.
Wagner, Carl R.
Walden, William T.
Waldroupe, Rick
Walker, J. L.
Walker, Jimmy
Walker, Johnny L.
Walker, L. L.
Wall, Richard L.
Wallace, Billy J.
Wallace, Wayne
Walter, C. A., Jr.
Walters, Billy E.
Walters, John Paul
Walters, Maxie E.
Walton, Richard R.
Walton, Shirley V.
Ward, Carolyn Jo
Ward, Darrell N.
Ward, Dorothy L.
Ward, Herbert R.
Ward, J. F.
Ward, M. Lajean
Warden, B. V.
Warden, Russell D.
Warren, Stanley G.
Wasson, Ronald E.
Waters, Cletis R.
Waters, John
Watson, Donald L
Watson, Freada A.
Watson, R. P.
Waugh, J. E.
Weaver, Robert E.
Webb, Carl Frank
Webb, Dexter
Webb, Thomas J.
Webster, H. J.
Wedgeworth, Ernest,
   Sr.
Welbern, Wendell H.
Welch, Troy L.
Wells, Elton T. Z.
Wells, Mary Ellen
Wells, R. L.
Welton, E. A.
Wensauer, D. F.
Werner, Frederick L.
West, Billy R.
West, C. L.
West, Jim
West, J. W.
West, L. D.
Westbrook, Josh L.
Whaley, Gertrude
Wheat, J. L.
Wheeler, E. E.
White, David
White, Gerald M.
White, Harry W.
White, Jack W.
White, Polly J.
White, R. L.
Whitehead, Esther
Whitehead, M. C.

Whitfill, David J.
Whitley, Ray L.
Whitman, R. E.
Whitmore, D. C.
Whitson, D. L.
Whitten, Joel A.
Whychell, Robert E.
Wiegert, Orval W.
Wiggins, A. P., Jr.
Wilbanks, Dortha F.
Wilbanks, Jo Ann
Wilbert, H. L.
Wilhelm, L. F.
Wilhite, K. D.
Wilkins, Gerald W.
Wilkinson, Betty K.
Wilkinson, F. E.
Wilkinson, V. L.
Williams, Alvin D.
Williams, Billy D.
Williams, C. L.
Williams, J. C., Jr.
Williams, L. Louise
Williams, Larry R.
Williams, Larry W.
Williams, Leon G.
Williams, P. H.
Williams, Paul D.
Williams, Paul H.
Williams, Roy L.
Willis, William A.
Willits, C. R.
Wilson, Charles L.
Wilson, E. W.
Wilson, Guy
Wilson, J. D.
Wilson, Patrick
Wilson, Tommy L.
Wilson, W. L.
Windle, J. M.
Windsor, J. C.
Wirth, David, Jr.
Wisdom, J. D.
Wojahn, W. L.
Wolfe, Charles R.
Wolfinger, Tommy R.
Womack, Donnie L.
Womack, James
Wood, Carlon E.
Woodard, Charles E.
Woodfork, Curtis E.
Woolever, Gerald T.
Wright, L. T.
Wright, Robert M.
Wright, Ronald L.
Wright, V. Gerald
Wright, M. A., Jr.
Wrigley, Joseph F.
Wyalie, B. J.
Wyatt, R. D.
Wynd, Eugene G.
Wyrick, Ronald G.
Wyskup, Lawrence
Yancey, Jerry J.
Yandell, James R.
Yeaman, Doug C.
Yeck, Delvin
Yerton, Walter S., Jr.
Yott, Arlis L.
Young, Billy G.
Young, Glenn T.
Young, Howard L.
Young, Lahoma
   Annette
Young, Lyndall R.
Young, William H.
Youngblood, E. R., Jr.

Special Thanks

are extended to the following contributors to *Our First 100 Years* and to the many other members and retirees who provided assistance.

Beverly Bennett, History Book
    Project Manager

Howard Brown

Bob Bunce

Corporate Communications staff

Charles Creech

Jean Dunkins

Irma Elliott

Thomas George

Ross Harlan

Harvey Harris

William Kirk

Grady Little

W.L. Magnus

Bill Moore

Steven E. Moore

Calvin Pryor

Allen Sadler

Jim Tabor

Centennial Steering Committee
    members:

Irma Elliott

Donald Rowlett

Dale Hennessy

Paul Renfrow

Centennial Committee members:

Brian Alford

Wayne Beasley

Laura Burgert

Bill Busch

Ruth Ann Chaffin

Belleva Johnson

Dwight Ponder

Judy Puckett

Rob Ratley

Rae Rice

Shawntrell Scott

About the Author

Robert R. Morris specializes in researching and writing institutional and organizational histories. He brings his love of history, his talent for writing, and his organizational skills to this highly specialized publishing niche.

The author of more than thirty books, Morris is a former high school teacher and administrator who left the halls of academe in 1990 to pursue his dream of writing. He wrote a regular newspaper column for ten years and has spent a considerable amount of time

working with nonprofit organizations and boards.

Married for thirty years, Morris and his wife have two grown sons and their passion is international travel. Morris lives and works in the Chicago area.